Caŋdī Homa Vidhānam

*

Dr. Ramamurthy N.

M.Sc., B.G.L., CAII B, CCP, DSADP, CISA, PMP, CGBL, Ph.D.

*

Title: *Caŋḍī Homa Vidhānam*

First Edition: 2022

Author: **Dr. Ramamurthy N**, Chennai.
http://ramamurthy.jaagruti.co.in/

Number of pages: 64

Price: ₹ 200.00

ISBN (13): 978-93-82237-92-1

Printed at:

Published by:

*****

Table of Contents

*****

உ
ப்ரஹ்மைவ ஸத்யம்
SRI SWAYAMPRAKASA AVADHUTHA SADASIVA TRUST

Sri Sri Judge Swamigal Adhishtanam, East 7th Street,
PUDUKKOTTAI-622 001
Phone: 04322-221440, 222128
Email: sribhuvaneshwari@gmail.com

Blessings

Date : 29/10/2022

ப்ரசண்ட3யதி விக்ரமம், ஜ2டிதி க2ண்ட3யத்யாபத3:
ஸ"மண்ட3யதி வாக்கலாம் ஸத3ஸி த3ண்ட3யத்யுத்3த4தான்
கரண்ட3யதி ரோத3ஸீ கு3ண-ஸம்ருத்3தி4பி4ர்யா ஹி தாம்
ப4ஜாமி ப4யக2ண்டி3காம் ஸபதி3 சண்டி3காமம்பி3காம்

மகிமைகள் நிறைந்த ஸ்துதியான ஸ்ரீ துர்கா ஸப்தசதி, வேத வ்யாஸர் படைத்த மார்க்கண்டேய புராணத்தில் 73வது அத்தியாயம் முதல் 85 வது அத்தியாயம் வரை மொத்தம் 13 அத்தியாயங்கள் உள்ள ஒரு பாகம். அம்பிகையின் பெருமையைச் சொல்வதால் தேவீ மஹாத்ம்யம் என்றும், சண்டிகா தேவியின் ப்ரபாவம் விளங்குவதால் "சண்டீ" என்றும் எழுநூறு மந்த்ரங்கள் அடங்கியதால் "ஸப்தசதி" என்றும் கூறப்படுகிறது.

புவனேச்வரி ஸம்ஹிதை **"யதாவேதோஹ்யனாதர்ஹி தத்வத் ஸப்தசதீ ஸ்ம்ருதா"** என்று வேதத்தைப் போலவே ஸப்தசதியும் அநாதி என்கிறது.

புராணாங்கமாயினும் ஸப்தசதி வேதத்தைப் போலவே பழமையானது. கிடைத்தற்கரியது.

மாஹாத்ம்யத்தின் ப்ரதம சரித்ரத்திற்கு ப்ரம்மா ருஷி. இது ருக்வேத ஸ்வரூபம். மத்யம சரித்ரத்திற்கு விஷ்ணு ருஷி. இது யஜுர் வேத ஸ்வரூபம். உத்தம சரித்ரத்தின் ருஷி ருத்ரன். இது ஸாமவேத ஸ்வரூபம். அதாவது ஸப்தசதியின் மூன்று சரித்ரங்களும் த்ரிமூர்த்திகளால் தோன்றியது. மூன்று வேதங்களின் வடிவம்.

ஸப்தசதி ப்ரதம சரித்ரத்தில் கர்ம காண்டம், மத்யம சரித்திரத்தில் உபாஸனா காண்டம், உத்தம சரித்ரத்தில் ஞான காண்டம் நிழல் போல் கோடிட்டுக் காட்டப்பட்டுள்ளன.

தேவீ மாஹாத்ம்யத்தில் ச்ருதி, ஸ்ம்ருதி, புராணம், தந்திரம், தரிசனங்களின் சாராம்சம் பொதிந்துள்ளது. எனவேதான் இதன் தத்துவம் அந்த பராசக்திக்கு மட்டுமே முழுமையாகத் தெரியும். விஷ்ணுவுக்கு மூன்றில் ஒரு பாகமும், பிரம்மாவுக்கு பாதி, வேத வியாசருக்கு நான்கில் ஒரு பாகம், மற்றவர்களுக்கு கோடியில் ஒரு பாகம் தெரியும் என்று மேரு தந்திரம் என்ற நூல் கூறுகிறது.

ஜாதவேதஸே என்று துர்க்கையை அக்னியாகவே காண்கிறது வேதம் ! தாம் அக்னிவர்ணாம் தபஸா ஜ்வலந்தீம் என்கிறது.

அப்படிப்பட்ட தேவீ மாஹாத்ம்யத்தால் அக்னிஸ்வரூபமான அம்பிகைக்கு நடத்தப்படும் ஆராதனையே சண்டி ஹோமம்.

"**ஆராதிதா ஸைவந்ருணாம் போக ஸ்வர்காபவர்க்கதா**" என்ற வாக்யப்படி சண்டியின் ஆராதனை ஸகல க்ஷேமங்களையும் தரவல்லது. இஹலோகத்தில் ஸகல அபீஷ்டங்களும் பெற்று மோக்ஷத்தையும் அடையலாம் என்பதில் சிறிதளவும் ஐயமில்லை. ஸுரதன் என்ற அரசன் ராஜ்யத்தை ஆண்டதும், ஸமாதி என்ற வைச்யன் ஞானத்தை அடைந்ததும் மாஹாத்ம்ய சரிதத்திலேயே வருகிறது.

இத்தகைய பெருமை இருக்கும் காரணத்தால் தான் ஸ்ரீ சாந்தானந்த மஹா ஸ்வாமிகளும் நமது புதுக்கோட்டை புவனேச்வரி ஸந்நிதியில், அஷ்டாதசபுஜ மஹாலக்ஷ்மி துர்க்கையை ஸ்தாபிதம் செய்து, அங்கே கோலாஹலமாக பல்லாயிரம் சண்டி பாராயணங்களும், சண்டி ஹோமங்களும் செய்து வந்தது குறிப்பிடத்தக்கது.

இவ்வளவு மஹிமை பொருந்திய சண்டி ஹோம விதானத்தை நமது ப்ரிய சிஷ்யர் முனைவர் ராமமூர்த்தி நூலாகத் தொகுத்து, வெளியிட இருப்பதை அறிந்து பெருமகிழ்ச்சி அடைகிறோம்.

இது சண்டி உபாஸகர்களுக்கும் சண்டி ஹோமம் செய்பவர்களுக்கும் மிகவும் உபயோகமாக இருக்கும் என்பதில் ஐயமில்லை.

இந்நூலாசிரியர் ஸ்ரீ ராமமூர்த்தி அவர்களுக்கும் அவரது குடும்பத்தாருக்கும் இந்நூலினை படித்து இன்புறும் எல்லா பக்தர்களும், நமது மனமார்ந்த வாழ்த்துக்களும் ஆசிகளோடு, அஷ்டாதசபுஜ மஹாலக்ஷ்மியின் அருளும், ஸ்ரீபுவனேச்வரியின் அருளும், ஸத்குரு ஸ்ரீ சாந்தானந்த மஹாஸ்வாமிகளின் அருளும் பெற்று ஸுகானந்த ஸுகவாழ்வு கிடைத்திட ஜகன்மாதா ஸ்ரீ புவனேச்வரி தேவியை பிரார்த்தித்து ஆசிர்வதிக்கிறேன்.

ஆனந்தம் சுபம் மங்களம் ! ஜய புவனேச்வரி!

ஸ்ரீ ப்ரணவாநந்த ஸ்வாமின:
ஸ்ரீ புவனேச்வரி அவதூத வித்யா பீடம்
புதுக்கோட்டை

*****

Introduction

ॐ श्री गुरुभ्यो नमः । *Oṃ Śrī Gurubhyo Namaḥ* ।

गुरुर्ब्रह्मा गुरुर्विष्णुः गुरुर्देवो महेश्वरः । गुरु साक्षात् परं ब्रह्म तस्मै श्रीगुरवे नमः ॥

Gururbrahma Gururviṣṇuḥ Gururdevo Maheśvaraḥ ।
Guru Sākśāt Parabrahma Tasmai Śrīgurave Namaḥ ॥

गुरुवे सर्वलोकानां भिषजे भवरोगिनां । निधये सर्व विद्यानां दक्षिणा मूर्तये नमः ॥

Guruve Sarvloksansam Bhiṣaje Bhavaroginām ।

Nidhaye Sarva Vidhyānām Dakśiṇa Mūrtaye Namaḥ ॥

सदाशिव समारंभां शङ्कराचार्य मध्यमां। अस्मद आचार्य पर्यन्तां वन्दे गुरु परंपराम् ॥

Sadāshiva Samārambām Śankarāchārya Madhyamām ।

Asmad Achārya Paranthām Vande Guru Paramparām ॥

श्रुति स्मृति पुराणानामालयं करुणालयम् । नमामि भगवत्पादंशंकरं लोकशंकरम् ॥

Śruti Smruti Purānānām Ālayam Karunālayam ।
Namāmi Bhagavatapādam Śankaram Lokaśankaram ॥

वागर्थाविव सम्प्रुक्तौ वागर्थ प्रतिपत्तये । जगतः पितरौ वन्दे पार्वती परमेश्वरौ ॥

Vāgarthāviva Sampruktakou Vāgartha Pratipaye ।

Jagataḥ Pitarou Vande Pārvati Parameśwarou ॥

We all originated from *Brahmam*[1]. We reach that *Brahmam* – merge with that *Brahmam*. That is actually *lia-samāti*. This rhythm cannot be exercised without the use or support of an appropriate instructor. The *Upasana* is aimed at an idol. It is both *Suguna* (with qualities) and (without qualities) *Nirguna*. A person is capable of doing *Nirguna Upasana* only after he has attained *Sagunopasana*. Suddenly, it is impossible for one to get involved in *Nirgunobasana* straight away.

As mentioned in *Brahadāranyaka Upanishat* the *Ādhi Moolam*, also called as *Parabrahmam*, does not have any form or qualities. It does not fit within any limitations. However, in order to realise that *Brahmam* without any form, a sort of image worship is suggested. Once the maturity (*Sāloka, Sāmeepya* and *Sāyujya*) is reached, there is no need for any prescriptions

[1] *Brahmam* is different Lord *Brahma*. *Brahma* is the head of all Devas. On the other hand *Brahmam* is *Parabrahmam*, the supreme.

and/ or restrictions to worship gods with different images, fasting, etc. Various *karmas* have to be performed to take us to this *yogic* position.

Shiva, Shakti and *Vishnu* are all one and the same. These three Gods are without origin. For all other Gods we could read the origin and for some even the end could also be seen in one or other *Purana* or stories.

In the form of *Arddhanāreeshwara* the left half of Lord *Shiva* is *Shakti*. Again, in the form of *Shankaranārāyana*, the left half of Lord *Shiva* is *Vishnu*. This clearly evidences that *Shakti* and *Vishnu* are one and the same and naturally *Shiva* also.

Brahadāranyaka Upanishat verses (I–3, I–4), starting from *"Ātmaivetamagra Āseet"* till *"Sa Imamevātmānam Tvetāpātayat Tataḥ"* describes in this manner – the *Parabrahmam* seems to be two as husband and wife.

The energy of the *Parabrahmam* is *Sri Devi – Shakti*. Even when the power of that object is within it, the power cannot exist without the entity. Hence, the *Parabrahmam* is the *Shakti* and the *Shakti* is the *Parabrahmam*. Both cannot be different.

In the same manner, if *Eshwar* is considered as *Brahmam*, Goddess Ambika is merged with that *Eshwaran*. Can the fragrant and the flower be separate? How about whiteness and the milk? *Ambika* is thus unsplittable from *Eswaran*. *Parameswara* and *Parāshakti* are the earliest/ first couple to be inseparable; They are the mother and father of all living beings. Yet they are one and the same.

Chāndogya Upanishat (6:2:1) says *"Ekam Evātvetīyam"* – That is, all the Gods are the same – there is only one God, no two. *Brahma Sootram* says *"Ekam Brahma Dvitīya Nāste Neha Naye Nāste Naya Kinchana"* – there is only one God – no two – not at all two. *Yajur Veda* (32-3) utters – *"Na Tasya Pratimāsti Śutāma Pāpvitam"* – He is so holy and does not have any image.

Jagadguru Sri Adi Shankara Bhagavat Pada divided our *Sanatana* Hindu religion into six branches – sub-religions and established *Shanmathas* – *Gānapatyam, Koumaram, Shaivam, Vaishnavam, Shaktam* and Souram. *Adi Shankara*, though equally treated all these six sub-religions, he had a distinct admiration for Shaktam-Shakti. She is *Jaganmata* – the mother of this universe – the mother of all living beings.

We are not yet mature enough to realise the formless *Parabrahmam* (no need of writing/ reading this book, if we are that much mature).

Someone has to hold back or attach side wheels until one learns to drive a bicycle. Once he becomes expert these are not needed. We need a boat to cross a river. Once we have reached the other shore, what is the need of a boat.

Therefore, until we all mature enough, we need to worship a God with form – why can't it be the holy mother – is it not that we get that much pleasure when we call mother as *'Amma'*?

Jaganmata, Paradevatai, Sri Devi is called Chandee because she destroyed the demons Chanda and Munda and. Sri Durga Saptashathee also known as Sri Devi Mahatmyam, is a stotram that tells her story. That stotra is also called as Chandi. It contains 700 Shlokas. These shlokas are themselves Mantras. The Homa performed with those mantras, is called Chandee Homam. It is a powerful homam performed on Goddess Chandi who is the mother of the world. This Homam is a boon to remove the evil eyes and doshas that prevent us from living a fulfilling life, to remove the curses on this and past lives and to purify both the body and the soul.

The author of this book has earlier published a book titled "Sri Devi Stutigal" explaining the detailed recitation of Sri Devi Mahatmya Shlokas. This book is being written because the readers who have read it have been asked to know more about Chandi Homam. Chandi Homa is often performed in Tantric style. In some places it is also done according to Vedic method. All these are tried to be explained in the following topics;

- Agnimukham – Vaidhīkam
- Agnimukham –Tāntrīkam
- Vaidhīkam or Tāntrīkam?
- Caŋdī Homam

Also included are hymns about Chandi below;

- Śrī Caṇḍī Prātaḥ Smaraṇam
- Śrī Caṇḍī Pāṭhaḥ
- Śrī Caṇḍikā Hṛdaya Stotram
- Bhāvanopaniṣat

The author's Sri Vidya Guru, Head of Pudukkottai Bhuvaneswari Mutt, Poojyasri Pranavananda Saraswathi Avadutha Swamiji, has led the way in writing many books. Without his blessings and guidance this book could not have been written.

A few related mantras are also indicated wherever possible. In general, all the *mantras* are supposed to be secretive. All the more about *Shakti* related *mantras*. Hence, they are to be got initiated by an appropriate teacher (*guru*) only, before trying to chant of to do *japam*.

Devotees are advised to consult a qualified scholar or guru, if they have any doubts about any mantras or worshipping methods mentioned in this book. It is highly suggested not to start recitation/ puja with half-knowledge and assuming the rest. Books can only be a reference guide, but cannot act as a teacher (*guru*).

Generally, it is very difficult to read Samskruta words in English with proper pronunciation. It is apt to read them in Samskruta script itself. But to benefit those who cannot read Samskruta script the *mantras* have been given in English also. The Samskruta words, when transliterated in English are given in *italics*. Also, whenever She denotes Goddess *Sri Devi*, it is written as **She** or **Her**. Normally diacritical marks will be used for transliteration of Samskruta words into English. But general readers are not fully conversant with diacritical marks and hence they find it difficult to read. Hence, it not been used in this book in normal texts. But for proper pronunciation it has been completely used in *mantras*.
This book is simultaneously written in Tamil also.

My humble *pranāms* to *Śrīśrī Pranavānanda Saraswathi Swamiji,* for his blessings and some pleasantries about this edition.

My sincere thanks are due to all those who supported in this noble cause of bring out this book. Attempts have been made to give this book as much error free as possible. Still if there are any errors, apologies are sought. If the errors are given as feedback, it will the next edition to be fault free. Hope the readers would be benefitted by the contents of this book. The readers are requested to feel free to send their feedback and comments.

There is no doubt that *Sri Chandi Devī* will shower her compassion and blessings to all those who read this book.

Our humble *Praṇāms* to all our *Gurus*.

Om Tat Sat

Chennai
2022

Dr. Ramamurthy N

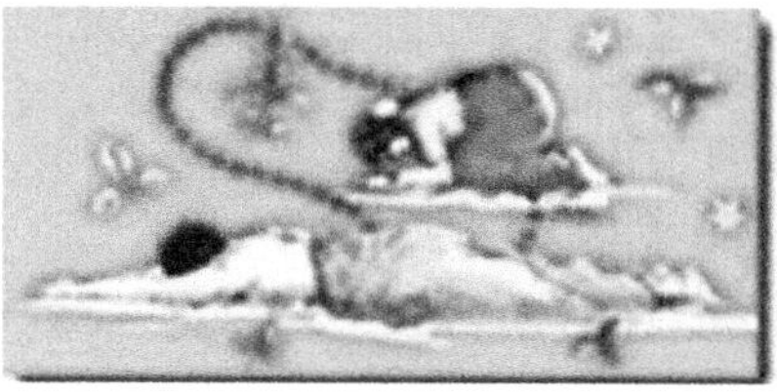

Agnimukham – Vaidhīkam

Mukha means mouth in Sanskrit. This can mean the mouth of Lord Agni.

To begin with;

- Anugnai – getting permission to perform havan.
- Ganapati Puja
- Punyagavacanam
- Kalasa Sthapanam
- Kalasa Puja

Whichever deity for whom the Homa is performed, keep the kalasam, invoke and worship Varuna in the kumba water and then invoke and worship the respective deity(ies).

In the same way, Agni Bhagavan has to established in the fire and worshiped and related samskaras have to be performed and then poorvangam. This is called Agnimukham. It is of two types – Vedic and Tantric. In this chapter we will see Vedic Agnimukham. In the next chapter the Tantric Agnimukham is discussed.

Later in a chapter the difference between Vedic and Tantric methods and which one should be used where and by whom are all discussed.

(It is a very big challenge to write this chapter in English – since there is no English equivalent for most of the Samskruta Words).

Vedic Agnimukham

1. At the place where the Agni is to be established, mark a square of ground with white rice flour, draw three lines from west to east (starting from south and ending at north) and three lines from south to north (starting from west and ending at east) with two darbas (as per the diagram below), touch the water and throw the darbas in south-west direction. Touch the water again.

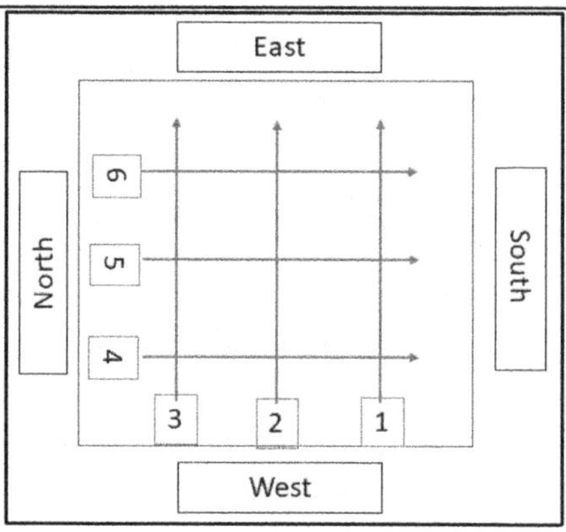

Normally the Agni is brought by the Sumangali ladies – usually the wife of the master performing the homam. In some places two ladies will bring the fire.

Note – Not sure if readers have noticed – Agni should be brought by the bridegroom's mother-in-law at the time of marriage.

2. The Agni thus brought should be consecrated in the Agni Kundam by saying "भूर्भुवस्सुवरोम् – *Bhoorbhuvassuvarom*". Add some akshatha and water to the vessel in which the Agni was brought by the ladies. Then pour out the rest of the water and take some other water and place it in the East direction. Light the fire and let it burn well.

3. *Paristharana* should be done with darbas from east of Agni in the circumambulation. The darbas in the East and West should have the North tip and the Darbhas in the North and South should have the East tip. The one in the South should be above the West-one and the one in the North should be below. 16 Dharbas should be used for each *parishtharana*.

To the North of Agni and *Paristharan*, Darbas should be spread in two rows of 12 each;

- Main Dharvi[2] and ghee vessel
- Prokshanee's vessel and Pranitha vessel
- Other Dharvi and Idmam[3]

[2] Dharvi is the spoon used to take ghee and pour in the fire. It can be mango leaf, bay leaf, or wooden spoon.

[3] 3 for parithi, 2 for food, 15 for homam, one for upastharana – hence a total of 21 samittus is called Idmam.

To the west of the Agni and Paristharana, (to the east of the Acharya) spread 12 darbhas and place the ghee vessel and the Prokshanee vessel on it.

Note: Only *Paristi* and Agni Kundam can be inside Paristarana.

4. Make a *pavitram* on a piece of dung with two darbas whose tip is not damaged, touch the water and touch the vessels with that pavitram. Take the *proshanee* vessel and place it on the tarps spread to the west of Agni and *Parastharana* add some Akshatha and water to it and sanctify it from west to east with pavitram. Keep the vessels upright, untie the *samittu* bundle and propitiate the water with the sanctity. Keep plenty of water on the right side.

5. Take the *praneetha* vessel and place it on the Darbas spread to the west of Agni. Add some Akshatha and water to it and sanctify it from west to east with the *pavitram*. The vessel is lifted up to the tip of the nose and then placed on the *darbai* to the North of the fire, covered with two other darbas and say "वरुणाय नमः सकलाराधनैः स्वर्चितम् । *Varunāya Namaḥ. Sakalārādhanaiḥ Svarchitam* – Salutations to Lord Varuna, be well-worshipped in all respects.

6. On the darbas spread to the South of Agni and Paristharana, place a *koorcham* or a coconut as Brahma and recite ""अस्मिन् होमकर्मणि ब्रह्माणं त्वां वृणे । ब्रह्मणे नमः सकलाराधनैः स्वर्चितम् । *Asmin Hōma Karmaṇi Prahmāṇam Tvām Vruṇē. Brahmane Namaḥ. Sakalārādhanaiḥ Svarchitam*" – Salutations to Lord *Brahma*, be well worshiped in all respects.

Some refer one Acharya himself as Brahma. If not, a *koorcham* or coconut can be used.

7. Melt the ghee in a different fire and place the *pavithram* in the center of the ghee bowl and fill it with ghee. Keep it in a separate fire to the North of Homa Kundam. Dip two darba tips in water and put them in the ghee. Show the tips of the one darba on fire and show to the ghee bowl and throw it in South-west direction. Again, show the tips of the two darbas on fire and show the flame three times around the ghee and throw them towards the North. Lower the ghee vessel in the north side and merge the fire to the main Agni. Then, keeping the vessel upright, clean it three times with the pavithram, from west to east and from east to west, untie the knot of the pavithram, touch it with water and add it to the fire.

8. Show both the *homa* spoons (*dharvi*) to the fire, wipe it up and down with darbai, show it again to the fire, sprinkle some water, keep them down, touch the water and put the *darbai* in the fire.

Note – So far, we have cleaned everything to be used for the homa and placed it in the appropriate places. Homam begins now.

9. *Parishesanam* – अदितेऽनुमन्यस्व । अनुमतेऽनुमन्यस्व । सरस्वतेऽनुमन्यस्व । देव सवितः प्रसुव ॥ *Atitēnumanyasva*| *Anumatēnumanyasva*| *Sarasvatēnumanyasva* | *Dēvasavitaḥ Prasuva* ||

Take the water in the hands and sprinkle around the Agni on the South, West and North sides, from the north-east corner to *pradakshina* and again to the North-east corner. *Aditi Devi*, Mother of Devas! grant permission (to perform Homam). May the goddess of permission grant permission (to do homam). May the Goddess Saraswathi grant permission (to perform Homam). Savitru Deva! Bless us all.

10. *Agni Dhyanam* – Meditate on Lord Agni by chanting the mantra below;

चत्वारि शृंगा त्रयो अस्य पादा द्वे शीर्षे सप्तहस्तासो अस्य । त्रिधा बद्धो वृषभो रोरवीति महो देवो मर्त्यां आविवेश । एष हि देवः प्रदिशोऽनु सर्वाः पूर्वो हि जातः स उ गर्भे अन्तः । स वि जायमानः स जनिष्यमाणः प्रत्यङ्मुखास्तिष्ठति विश्वतोमुखः ॥

Beginning from the East of Agni has to be decorated on all sides with Akshadai as per below mantra;

प्राङ्मुखो देव हे अग्ने अभिमुखो भव ॥ अग्न्यलंकरणम् । इन्द्राय नमः । अग्नये नमः । यमाय नमः । निर्ऋतये नमः । वरुणाय नमः । वायवे नमः । सोमाय नमः । ईशानाय नमः । अग्नये नमः । आत्मने नमः । सर्वेभ्यो ब्राह्मणेभ्यो नमः ॥

11. Idmam – Samittu – " अस्मिन् होम-कर्मणि ब्रह्मन् इद्मातास्ये | *Asmiṉ Hōma-Karmaṇi Brahmaṉ Idmātāsyē* |" – O Brahma, in this Homa Karma, permit me to add *Idmam* to Agni. He says " ॐ आधत्स्व | – Om *Ādhatsva* |" After getting that permission, keep one of the remaining 16 samittus in the North for *upasthana* and dip the other 15 samittus in the ghee and add them to the fire.

12. Taking ghee with the small *Dharvi* (spoon) and meditating on *Prajapati* in mind, do homam so that the ghee falls continuously from the North-west corner to the South-east corner of the Agni Kund – "स्वाहा। प्रजापतय इदं न मम ॥ – *Svāhā / Prajāpataya Idam Na Mama* ॥ This is Prajapati's and not mine.

13. Similarly, taking ghee with a large *dharvi* and meditating on Indra in mind, do homam so that the ghee falls continuously from the South-west corner to the north-east corner of the Agni Kund – "स्वाहा। इंद्राय इदं न मम ॥ – *Svāhā* | *Indrāya Idam Na Mama* ॥" This is Indra's and not mine.

14. *Ājyabhāgam – by the bigger Dharvi;*

- अग्नये स्वाहा । अग्नय इदं न मम ॥ *Agṉayē Svāhā* (in the north-east half) *Agnaya Idam Na Mama* ॥ It is Agni's and not mine.
- सोमाय स्वाहा । सोमाय इदं न मम ॥ *Somāya Svāhā* (in the south-east half) *Somāya Idam Na Mama* ॥ It is *Soman*'s and not mine.
- संकल्प प्रभृति एतक्षण पर्यन्तं मध्ये संभावित समस्त दोष प्रायश्चित्तार्थं सर्व प्रायश्चित्तं होष्यामि। ओं भूर्भुवस्सुवः स्वाहा । प्रजापतय इदं न मम ॥ *Saṅkalpa Prabhruti Ētakṣaṇa Paryantam Madhyē Sambhāvita Samasta Dōṣa Prāyaścittārtam Sarva Prāyaścittam Hōṣyāmi* | *Ōm Bhūrbhuvas'suvaḥ Svāhā* | *Prajāpataya Idam Na Mama* ॥

I perform this homam as a propitiation for all the errors and mistakes that happened between the time of Sankalpam and this moment. It is Prajapati's and not mine.

So far, the prelude to homa has been explained. The above is common to any homam pertaining to any God. Now let us start doing the main homam.

Main Homam

Now we can start doing the main homam. Since the scope of this book is about Chandi Homam, it has been explained in detail in a separate chapter.

Uttarāṅkam

"Ētat Karma Samrudyartham Jayādi Hōmam Kariṣyē" – thus making the sankalpam, ghee is offered for 53 times in the Agni to all kinds of deities starting from *Pitrus.*

Then complete the homam by performing the *ahudis* mentioned below;

प्रजापते न त्वदेतान्यन्यो विश्वा जातानि परि ता बभूव ।
यत्कामास्ते जुहुमस्तन्नो अस्तु वयꣳ स्याम पतयो रयीणाꣳ स्वाहा ।
प्रजापत्य इदम् ॥ ॥

कृद्विद्वान सर्वꣳ स्विष्टꣳ सुहुतं करोतु स्वाहा । अग्नये स्विष्टकृत इदम ॥

54. *Prajāpati*! The whole world has appeared from you. We do homam for you. Do fulfill our desires. We want to become rich.

58. Agni deva, who is the all-knowing and perfecting-performer of this *karma*, should make it suitable and well-provided. It belongs to Agni Deva who is known as *'Svishtakrut'*.

Anākñāta Prāyaccittam

प्राणानायम्य। अस्मिन् कर्मणि अविज्ञातप्रायश्चित्तादीनि करिष्ये।
अनाज्ञातं यदाज्ञातं यज्ञस्य क्रियते मिथु । अग्ने तदस्य कल्पय त्वꣳ हि
वेत्थ यथातथं स्वाहा । अग्नय इदम् ॥ १ ॥

1. Do *Pranāyāma*. I am making atonement for the crimes committed knowingly or unknowingly. Lord Agni! Knowingly or unknowingly, any deficiency in this worship should be treated as complete. You know best what and how it should be.

पुरुषसंमितो यज्ञो यज्ञः पुरुषसंमितः । अग्ने तदस्य कल्पय त्वꣳहि वेत्थ यथातथं स्वाहा । अग्नय इदम् ॥ २ ॥

यत्पाकत्रा मनसा दीनदक्षा न । यज्ञस्य मन्वते-मर्तासः । अग्निष्टद्धोता क्रतुविद्विजानन् यजिष्ठो देवान् ऋतुशोयजाति स्वाहा । अग्नय इदम् ॥ ३ ॥

2. Oh Lord Agni! *Yajna* is equivalent to *Paramapurusha*. The *yajna* was ordained by *Paramapurusha* himself. Its ritual should be completed. You know best what and how it should be.

3. People, who are narrow-minded and incompetent who do not know the philosophy of *Yajna*, who knows it and conducts the Yajna with complete understanding and summoner of the Gods, Agni Deva should conduct the worship of the Gods in the appropriate manner at the respective times.

भूः स्वाहा । अग्नय इदम् ॥ ४ ॥

भुवः स्वाहा । वायव इदम् ॥ ५ ॥

सुवः स्वाहा । सूर्यायेदं न मम ॥ ६ ॥

अस्मिन् होमकर्मणि मध्ये संभावित समस्तदोषप्रायश्चित्तार्थं सर्वप्रायश्चित्तं होष्यामि । ओंभूर्भुवःसुवः स्वाहा । प्रजापतय इदं न मम ॥ ७ ॥

श्रीविष्णवे स्वाहा । विष्णवे परमात्मन इदम् ॥ ८ ॥

नमो रुद्राय पशुपतये स्वाहा । रुद्राय पशुपतय इदं न मम ॥ (अप उपस्पृश्य) ॥ ९ ॥

4. This *āhudi* is for the *vyāhruti* called *'Bhooḥ'*. It belongs to Agni and not mine.

5. This *āhudi* is for the *vyāhruti* called *'Bhuvaḥ'*. It belongs to *Vāyu* and not mine.

6. This *āhudi* is for the *vyāhruti* called *'Suvaḥ'*. It belongs to Sun God and not mine.

7. Even in this *Karma* whatever has been deficient may Agni deva, the All-Knowing and Completion-of-defects, make it suitable and well-provided.

8. It belongs to Sri Vishnu and not mine.

9. It belongs to *Pasupathi Rudra* and not to me. (Touch the water)

59. The arcs should be touched with ghee and first the middle arc and then the other two arcs should be added to the fire. "ॐ भूर्भुवस्सुवः स्वाहा । प्रजापतय इदं न मम ॥ *Om Bhūrbhuvas'suvaḥ Svāhā* I *Prajāpataya Idam Na Mama* ॥
"Homam should be performed with ghee as continuous flow along with both *Dharvis*. May it be well-offered to the *'Samsrava'* part – the *Vasus*, the *Rudras* and the *Ādityas*.

सप्त ते अग्ने समिधस्सप्तजिह्वास्सप्तऋषय - स्सप्तधामप्रियाणि । सप्तहोत्रा स्सप्तधा त्वा यजन्ति सप्तयोनीरापृणस्वघृतेन स्वाहा । अग्नये सप्तवत इदम् ॥ १० ॥

10. Oh Agni God! Seven *samitus*, seven tongues, seven rishis, seven beloved abodes, seven *hotas* worship You in seven kinds of *Yajna*. Fill your *moolasthana* with ghee (keep both Dharvis in the right hand and perform *Poornahudi* homam with the ghee falling continuously from the vessel in the left hand). Place the tips of the two dharpas placed earlier in the ghee bowl on the fire. It belongs to Agni Deva who is in seven forms. And not mine.

आज्यस्थालीमुत्तरतो निधाय । प्राणानायम्य । अदिते-ऽन्वमꣳस्थाः । अनुमतेऽन्वमꣳस्थाः । सरस्वतेऽन्वमꣳस्थाः । देव सवितः प्रासावीः ॥ ११ ॥

11. Do *pranayama* by keeping the ghee vessel in the north and do *parshesana* for the Agni. Goddess Aditi, you blessed me to complete this homam well. O Goddess of permission, you have graced me to complete this homam well. Goddess Saraswathi, you blessed me to complete this homam well. Lord Savitr, you have blessed me to complete this homam well.

12. "वरुणाय नमः सकलाराधनैः स्वर्चितम् I *Varunāya Namaḥ. Sakalārādhanaiḥ Svarchitam* – Salutations to Lord Varuna, be well-worshipped in all respects. Varuna was earlier invoked in the *Pranitha* vessel to the north of Agni. Pour some Akshat into it. Take the vessel and keep it in front (to the west of Agni), add some water, pour some water from it with the right hand in the east, south, west, north and into it and let the rest of the water slide down. Purify self and everyone by sprinkling that water.

13. For the Brahma south of Agni "ब्रह्मन् वरन्ते ददामि I ब्रह्मणे नमः सकलाराधनैः स्वर्चितम् | *Brahman Varande Dadāmi. Brahmane Namaḥ. Sakalārādhanaiḥ Svarchitam*" – Salutations to Lord *Brahma*, be well worshiped in all respects. – I offer you the best offerings.

14.

प्रागादिपरिस्तरणमुत्तरे विसृजेत् ॥ १४ ॥

स्वाहा । अग्नेरुपस्थानं करिष्ये ॥

Add the *paristaranams* in the East etc., sides to the North. Say "स्वाहा – *Svāhā*" and add the one Samittu which was kept in the North earlier to Agni. "*Agne Upasthānam Karishye*" – Say this mantra by standing up.

अग्ने नय सुपथा राये अस्मान् विश्वानि देव वयुनानि विद्वान् । युयोध्यस्मज्जुहुराण - मेनो भूयिष्ठान्ते नम उक्तिं विधेम अग्नये नमः । अग्निं आत्मन्युद्वासयामि । हृदये अञ्जलिं दद्यात् ॥ १५॥

15. O Agni! guide us in a good way to enjoy wealth (due to our actions). God knows all thoughts. God! You know all thoughts. You will destroy the sin that hides and corrupts. We offer obeisance to you.

Do Anjali by saying "I make Agni rise again in the soul".

नमस्ते गार्हपत्याय नमस्ते दक्षिणाग्नये । नम आहवनीयाय महावेद्यै नमो नमः ॥

काण्डद्वयोपपाद्याय कर्मब्रह्म स्वरूपिणे । स्वर्गापवर्ग रूपाय यज्ञेशाय नमो नमः ॥

यज्ञेशाच्युत गोविन्द माधवानन्त केशवः । कृष्ण विष्णो हृषीकेश वासुदेव नमोऽस्तु ते ॥ १६

16. Salutations to you, the *Kārhabatyāgni*. Salutations to you, the *Dakshi-Nāgni*. Salutations to you, the *Āhavaneeyāgni*. Salutations to *Mahāvedi*. Salutations to *Yajneshvara*, who is worshiped by both kandas, who is in the form of karma and in the form of Brahma, who is in the form of heaven and in the form of *moksha*. *Yagneshā*! *Achyutā*! *Govindā*! *Mādavā*! *Anantā*! *Keshavā*! *Krishnā*! *Vishnu*! *Hrishikeshā*! *Vāsudevā*! Salutations to you".

Lebakaryam

Only if *Anna* (rice) Homam is performed, Lebakaryam should be performed – Place the big *dharvi* on the right side of the ghee bowl and the small *dharvi* in the middle. Take the *darbais* kept under the vessels, touch the big dharvi with the tip, the small dharvi in the middle and the ghee bowl with bottom – likewise three times. Keeping one *darbai* in the lap and the others, should be added to Agni. Again, touch the water and add the *darbai* kept in the lap to the fire. Point three fingers and chant Agni *Abhimantram* and touch the earth.

समर्पणम् ॥

कायेन वाचा मनसेन्द्रियैर्वा बुद्ध्यात्मना वा प्रकृतेः स्वभावात् ।
करोमि यद्यत् सकलं परस्मै नारायणायेति समर्पयामि ॥ १९ ॥

मन्त्रहीनं क्रियाहीनं .....

अभिवादये ..... नमस्कारः ॥

With deficiency, in chanting the *Mantras*, doing the *Kriyas*, without *Bhakti*, whatever Homam was performed by me should be made perfect. Be it prayer, penance, blackness, whatever, the head is best, if you think of Sri Krishna.

Whatever I do with my body, speech, mind, *Karma* organs, *Gnana* organs, or the movement of nature, I submit everything to the Lord *Narayana*.

Abhivādaye ..... Namaskāraḥ ॥

रक्षा । बृहत् साम क्षत्रभृद्वृद्धवृष्णियं त्रिष्टुभौजश्शुभित-

मुग्रवीरम् । इन्द्र स्तोमेन पञ्चदशेन मध्यमिदं वातेन सगरेण रक्ष ॥१८॥

May the *Bruhatsama Mantra*, which preserves strength, develops virility, bestows *dharana* energy and supreme welfare, warrior sons, in the form of Drushtup Chandas, protect us. Lord Indra! Wait for this body that appears between the two periods.

Take some *darba*, flower, *akshatai* and water and surround the fire saying "*Idanīm Agnim Āvāhita Samasta Devatām, Kumbe Arpayāmi*" and add all the deities who have been in the agni so far, to the *kumbha*.

Then complete the Pooja again to the deities in the Kumbha. Do not perform *Yatāsthanam* to the deities in the Kumbha if *abhishekam* of the Kumbha water is to be done to the idols of other deities. To perform *abhishekam* for human beings, *Yatāsthanam* to the deities in the Kumbha need to be done.

*****

Agnimukham –Tāntrīkam

1. At the place where the Agni is to be established, mark a square of ground with white rice flour, show *Avakundana*[4] *Mudra* with *'Hoom' beeja-aksharam* (root letter). It is ideal to have a one-inch-high platform. Draw three lines from west to east (starting from south and ending at north) and three lines from south to north (starting from west and ending at east) with two darbas (as per the diagram below), touch the water and throw the darbas in south-west direction. Touch the water again.

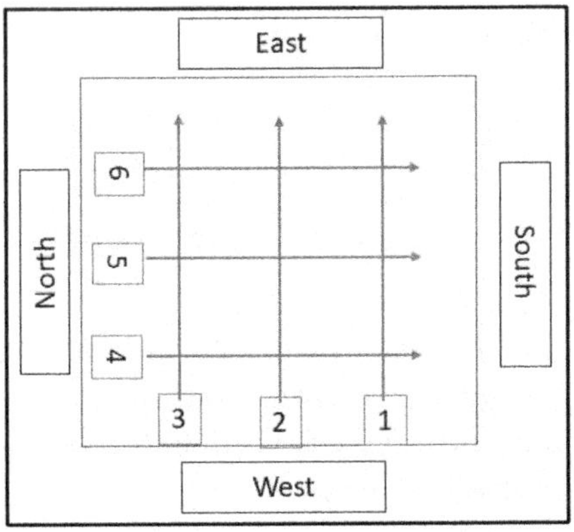

Pray in the order the lines were drawn – *Brahmaṇē Namaḥ, Yamāya Namaḥ, Sōmāya Namaḥ, Rudrāya Nama, Viṣṇavē Namaḥ* and *Indrāya Namaḥ.*

Consecrate the platform with the same Anganyasa Mantras in the South-east, North-East, South-west and North-west corners, middle and ends. Draw on it the Agni Chakra with octagon, hexagon and triangle in order of entry from outside to inside. Consecrate as clock-wise around the triangle in the eight directions and in the middle starting in front of self.

Normally the Agni is brought by the Sumangali ladies – usually the wife of the master performing the homam. In some places two ladies will bring the fire.

Note – Not sure if readers have noticed – Agni should be brought by the bridegroom's mother-in-law at the time of marriage.

---

[4] Avakundanam is to circumnavigate the Agni Kundam in clock-wise and anti-clockwise, with the right hand and then with the left hand, with the index fingers extended into fists.

2. The Agni thus brought should be consecrated in the Agni Kundam by saying "भूर्भुवस्सुवरोम् – *Bhoorbhuvassuvarom*". Add some akshatha and water to the vessel in which the Agni was brought by the ladies. Then pour out the rest of the water and take some other water and place it in the East direction. Light the fire and let it burn well.

3. *Paristharana* should be done with darbas from east of Agni in the circumambulation. The darbas in the East and West should have the North tip and the Darbhas in the North and South should have the East tip. The one in the South should be above the West-one and the one in the North should be below. 16 Dharbas should be used for each *parishtharana*.

To the North of Agni and *Paristharan*, Darbas should be spread in two rows of 12 each;

- Main Dharvi[5] and ghee vessel
- *Prokshanee's* vessel and *Pranitha* vessel
- Other *Dharvi* and *Idmam*[6]

To the west of the Agni and Paristharana, (to the east of the Acharya) spread 12 darbhas and place the ghee vessel and the Prokshanee vessel on it.

Note: Only *Pariti* and Agni Kundam can be inside Paristarana.

4. Make a *pavitram* on a piece of dung with two darbas whose tip is not damaged, touch the water and touch the vessels with that pavitram. Take the *proshanee* vessel and place it on the tarps spread to the west of Agni and *Parastharana* add some Akshatha and water to it and sanctify it from west to east with pavitram. Keep the vessels upright, untie the *samittu* bundle and propitiate the water with the sanctity. Keep plenty of water on the right side.

5. Take the *praneetha* vessel and place it on the Darbas spread to the west of Agni. Add some Akshatha and water to it and sanctify it from west to east with the *pavitram*. The vessel is lifted up to the tip of the nose and then placed on the *darbai* to the North of the fire, covered with two other

[5] Dharvi is the spoon used to take ghee and pour in the fire. It can be mango leaf, bay leaf, or wooden spoon.

[6] 3 for parithi, 2 for food, 15 for homam, one for upastharana – hence a total of 21 samittus is called Idmam.

darbas and say "वरुणाय नमः सकलाराधनैः स्वर्चितम् । *Varunāya Namaḥ. Sakalārādhanaiḥ Svarchitam* – Salutations to Lord Varuna, be well-worshipped in all respects.

6. On the darbas spread to the South of Agni and Paristharana, place a *koorcham* or a coconut as Brahma and recite ""अस्मिन् होमकर्मणि ब्रह्माणं त्वां वृणे । ब्रह्मणे नमः सकलाराधनैः स्वर्चितम् । *Asmin Hōma Karmaṇi Prahmāṇam Tvām Vruṇē. Brahmane Namaḥ. Sakalārādhanaiḥ Svarchitam*" – Salutations to Lord *Brahma*, be well worshiped in all respects.

Some refer one Acharya himself as Brahma. If not, a *koorcham* or coconut can be used.

7. Melt the ghee in a different fire and place the *pavithram* in the center of the ghee bowl and fill it with ghee. Keep it in a separate fire to the North of Homa Kundam. Dip two darba tips in water and put them in the ghee. Show the tips of the one darba on fire and show to the ghee bowl and throw it in South-west direction. Again, show the tips of the two darbas on fire and show the flame three times around the ghee and throw them towards the North. Lower the ghee vessel in the north side and merge the fire to the main Agni. Then, keeping the vessel upright, clean it three times with the pavithram, from west to east and from east to west, untie the knot of the pavithram, touch it with water and add it to the fire.

8. Show both the *homa* spoons (*dharvi*) to the fire, wipe it up and down with darbai, show it again to the fire, sprinkle some water, keep them down, touch the water and put the *darbai* in the fire.

Note – So far, we have cleaned everything to be used for the homa and placed it in the appropriate places. Homam begins now.

9. *Parishesanam* – अदितेऽनुमन्यस्व । अनुमतेऽनुमन्यस्व । सरस्वतेऽनुमन्यस्व । देव सवितः प्रसुव ॥ *Atitēऽnumaṉyasva*। *Aṉumatēऽnumaṉyasva*। *Sarasvatēऽ-ṉumaṉyasva* । *Dēvasavitaḥ Prasuva* ॥

Take the water in the hands and sprinkle around the Agni on the South, West and North sides, from the north-east corner to *pradakshina* and again to the North-east corner. *Aditi Devi*, Mother of Devas! grant permission (to perform Homam). May the goddess of permission grant permission (to do homam). May the Goddess Saraswathi grant permission (to perform Homam). Savitr Deva! Bless us all.

10. *Agni Dhyanam* – Meditate on Lord Agni by chanting the mantra below;

चत्वारि शृंगा त्रयो अस्य पादा द्वे शीर्षे सप्तहस्तासो अस्य । त्रिधा बद्धो वृषभो रोरवीति महो देवो मर्त्यां॒ आविवेश । एष हि देवः प्रदिशोऽनु सर्वाः पूर्वो हि जातः स उ गर्भे अन्तः । स वि जायमानः स जनिष्यमाणः प्रत्यङ्मुखास्तिष्ठति विश्वतोमुखः ॥

Beginning from the East of Agni has to be decorated on all sides with Akshadai as per below mantra;

प्राङ्मुखो देव हे अग्ने अभिमुखो भव ॥ अग्न्यलंकरणम् । इन्द्राय नमः । अग्नये नमः । यमाय नमः । निर्ऋतये नमः । वरुणाय नमः । वायवे नमः । सोमाय नमः । ईशानाय नमः । अग्नये नमः । आत्मने नमः । सर्वेभ्यो ब्राह्मणेभ्यो नमः ॥

11. Idmam – *Samittu* – " अस्मिन् होम-कर्मणि ब्रह्मन् इध्मातास्ये | *Asmin̲ Hōma-Karmaṇi Brahman̲ Idmātāsyē* |" – O Brahma, in this Homa Karma, permit me to add *Idmam* to Agni. He says " ॐ आधत्स्व | – Om *Ādhatsva* |" After getting that permission, keep one of the remaining 16 samittus in the North for *upasthana* and dip the other 15 samittus in the ghee and add them to the fire.

12. Taking ghee with the small *Dharvi* (spoon) and meditating on *Prajapati* in mind, do homam so that the ghee falls continuously from the North-west corner to the South-east corner of the Agni Kund – "स्वाहा। प्रजापतय इदं न मम ॥ – *Svāhā* I *Prajāpataya Idam Na Mama* II This is Prajapati's and not mine.

Similarly, taking ghee with a large *dharvi* and meditating on Indra in mind, do homam so that the ghee falls continuously from the South-west corner to the north-east corner of the Agni Kund – "स्वाहा। इंद्राय इदं न मम ॥ – *Svāhā* I *Indrāya Idam Na Mama* ||" This is Indra's and not mine.

13. *Ājyabhāgam – by the bigger Dharvi;*

- अग्नये स्वाहा । अग्नय इदं न मम ॥ *Agn̲ayē Svāhā* (in the north-east half) *Agnaya Idam Na Mama* ॥ It is Agni's and not mine.
- सोमाय स्वाहा । सोमाय इदं न मम ॥ *Somāya Svāhā* (in the south-east half) *Somāya Idam Na Mama* ॥ It is *Soman*'s and not mine.
- संकल्प प्रभृति एतक्षण पर्यन्तं मध्ये संभावित समस्त दोष प्रायश्चित्तार्थं सर्व प्रायश्चित्तं होष्यामि। ओं भूर्भुवस्सुव: स्वाहा । प्रजापतय इदं न मम ॥ *Saṅkalpa Prabhruti Ētakṣaṇa Paryantam Madhyē Sambhāvita Samasta Dōṣa Prāyaścittārtam Sarva Prāyaścittam Hōṣyāmi* I *Ōm Bhūrbhuvas'suvaḥ Svāhā* I *Prajāpataya Idam Na Mama* ||

I perform this homam as a propitiation for all the errors and mistakes that happened between the time of Sankalpam and this moment. It is Prajapati's and not mine.

So far, the prelude to homa has been explained. The above is common to any homam pertaining to any God. Now let us start doing the main homam.

Main Homam

The way in which, invoking and Shodasha Upachara Pujas are performed in *Kalasam*, Shodasha Upachara Pujas should also be performed in Agni by invoking the integrated form of Maha Kali, Maha Lakshmi and Maha Saraswathi as Chandika Devi. Homam should be performed with Navaksharee Moola Mantra, Sri Devi Mahatmya 700 Mantras, using different *dravyams*. Since the scope of this book is about Chandi Homam, it has been explained in detail in a separate chapter.

Uttarāṅkam
An̲ākñāta Prāyaccittam

Then complete the homam by performing the *ahudis* mentioned below;

प्राणानायम्य। अस्मिन् कर्मणि अविज्ञातप्रायश्चित्तादीनि करिष्ये।

अनाज्ञातं यदाज्ञातं यज्ञस्य क्रियते मिथु। अग्ने तदस्य कल्पय त्वꣳहि वेत्थ यथातथं स्वाहा। अग्नय इदम्॥ १॥

17. Do *Pranāyāma*. I am making atonement for the crimes committed knowingly or unknowingly. Lord Agni! Knowingly or unknowingly, any deficiency in this worship should be treated as complete. You know best what and how it should be.

पुरुषसंमितो यज्ञो यज्ञः पुरुषसंमितः। अग्ने तदस्य कल्पय त्वꣳहि वेत्थ यथातथं स्वाहा। अग्नय इदम्॥ २॥

यत्पाकत्रा मनसा दीनदक्षा न। यज्ञस्य मन्वते-मर्तासः। अग्निष्टद्धोता क्रतुविद्विजानन् यजिष्ठो देवान् ऋतुशोयजाति स्वाहा। अग्नय इदम्॥ ३॥

18. Oh Lord Agni! *Yajna* is equivalent to *Paramapurusha*. The *yajna* was ordained by *Paramapurusha* himself. Its ritual should be completed. You know best what and how it should be.

19. People, who are narrow-minded and incompetent who do not know the philosophy of *Yajna*, who knows it and conducts the Yajna with complete understanding and summoner of the Gods, Agni Deva should conduct the worship of the Gods in the appropriate manner at the respective times.

भूः स्वाहा। अग्नय इदम्॥ ४॥

भुवः स्वाहा। वायव इदम्॥ ५॥

सुवः स्वाहा। सूर्यायेदं न मम॥ ६॥

अस्मिन् होमकर्मणि मध्ये संभावित समस्तदोषप्रायश्चित्तार्थं

सर्वप्रायश्चित्तं होष्यामि । ओंभूर्भुवःसुवः स्वाहा । प्रजापतय इदं न मम ॥ ७ ॥

श्रीविष्णवे स्वाहा । विष्णवे परमात्मन इदम् ॥ ८ ॥

नमो रुद्राय पशुपतये स्वाहा । रुद्राय पशुपतय इदं न मम ॥ (अप उपस्पृश्य) ॥ ९ ॥

20. This *āhudi* is for the *vyāhruti* called *'Bhooḥ'*. It belongs to Agni and not mine.

21. This *āhudi* is for the *vyāhruti* called *'Bhuvaḥ'*. It belongs to *Vāyu* and not mine.

22. This *āhudi* is for the *vyāhruti* called *'Suvaḥ'*. It belongs to Sun God and not mine.

23. Even in this *Karma* whatever has been deficient may Agni deva, the All-Knowing and Completion-of-defects, make it suitable and well-provided.

24. It belongs to Sri Vishnu and not mine.

25. It belongs to *Pasupathi Rudra* and not to me. (Touch the water)

सप्त ते अग्ने समिधस्सप्तजिह्वास्सप्तऋषयः - स्सप्तधामप्रियाणि । सप्तहोत्राः स्सप्तधा त्वा यजन्ति सप्तयोनीरापृणस्वघृतेन स्वाहा । अग्नये सप्तवत इदम् ॥ १० ॥

26. Oh Agni God! Seven *samitus*, seven tongues, seven rishis, seven beloved abodes, seven *hotas* worship You in seven kinds of *Yajna*. Fill your *moolasthana* with ghee (keep both dharvis in the right hand and perform *Poornahudi* homam with the ghee falling continuously from the vessel in the left hand). Place the tips of the two dharpas placed earlier in the ghee bowl on the fire. It belongs to Agni Deva who is in seven forms. And not mine.

Note: –

• Seven Samittus – Peepal, Fig, Purusu, Vanni, Vigangatam, Lotus Leaf, Trees struck by thunder
• Seven tongues – *Kāli, Karāli*, Manojava, Sulohita, Sudhumravarna, Spulingini, Vishvarusi
• Seven Rishis – Agastya, Atri, Bharadvajar, Bruhu, Kutsa, Vasishta, Vamadeva.
• Seven Favorite Places – In Soma Yaga the places belonging to 7 Agnis namely Ahavaniyam, Karhabatyam, Dakshinagni, Saphyam, Avasathyam, Prajahitam, Agneetriyam.
• Seven Hotas – (Purifiers – Hotas) Prasasta, Brahmanachamsee, Bodha, Neshta, Agneetrar, Achavagar.
• Seven Yagnas – Agnishdom, Adhyagnishdom, Ugdyam, Shodasee, Athiratram, Apthoryama, Vajapeyam.

आज्यस्थालीमुत्तरतो निधाय । प्राणानायम्य । अदिते- ऽन्वमꣳस्थाः । अनुमतेऽन्वमꣳस्थाः । सरस्वतेऽन्वमꣳस्थाः । देव सवितः प्रासावीः ॥ ११ ॥

27. Do *pranayama* by keeping the ghee vessel in the north and do *parshesana* for the Agni. Goddess Aditi, you blessed me to complete this homam well. O Goddess of permission, you have graced me to complete this homam well. Goddess Saraswathi, you blessed me to complete this homam well. Lord Savitr, you have blessed me to complete this homam well.

28. "वरुणाय नम: सकलाराधनै: स्वर्चितम् । *Varunāya Namaḥ. Sakalārādhanaiḥ Svarchitam* – Salutations to Lord Varuna, be well-worshipped in all respects. Varuna was earlier invoked in the *praneetha* vessel to the north of Agni. Pour some akshata into it. Take the vessel and keep it in front (to the west of Agni), add some water, pour some water from it with the right hand in the east, south, west, north and into it and let the rest of the water slide down. Purify self and everyone by sprinkling that water.

29. For the Brahma south of Agni "ब्रह्मन् वरन्ते ददामि । ब्रह्मणे नम: सकलाराधनै: स्वर्चितम् | *Brahman Varande Dadāmi. Brahmane Namaḥ. Sakalārādhanaiḥ*

Svarchitam" – Salutations to Lord *Brahma*, be well worshiped in all respects. – I offer you the best offerings.

30.

प्रागादिपरिस्तरणमुत्तरे विसृजेत् ॥ १४ ॥
स्वाहा । अग्नेरुपस्थानं करिष्ये ॥

Add the paristaranams in the East etc., sides to the North. Say "स्वाहा – *Svāhā*" and add the one Samittu which was kept in the North earlier to Agni. "*Agne Upasthānam Karishye*" – Say this mantra by standing up.

अग्ने नय सुपथा राये अस्मान् विश्वानि देव वयुनानि विद्वान् । युयोध्यस्मज्जुहुराण - मेनो भूयिष्ठान्ते नम उक्तिं विधेम अग्नये नमः । अग्निं आत्मन्युद्वासयामि । हृदये अञ्जलिं दद्यात् ॥ १५ ॥

31. O Agni! guide us in a good way to enjoy wealth (due to our actions). God knows all thoughts. God! You know all thoughts. You will destroy the sin that hides and corrupts. We offer obeisance to you.

Do Anjali by saying "I make Agni rise again in the soul".

नमस्ते गार्हपत्याय नमस्ते दक्षिणाग्नये । नम आहवनीयाय महावेद्यै नमो नमः ॥

काण्डद्वयोपपाद्याय कर्मब्रह्म स्वरूपिणे । स्वर्गापवर्ग रूपाय यज्ञेशाय नमो नमः ॥

यज्ञेशाच्युत गोविन्द माधवानन्त केशव: । कृष्ण विष्णो हृषीकेश वासुदेव नमोऽस्तु ते ॥ १६

32. Salutations to you, the *Kārhabatyāgni*. Salutations to you, the *Dakshi-Nāgni*. Salutations to you, the *Āhavaneeyāgni*. Salutations to *Mahāvedi*. Salutations to *Yajneshvara*, who is worshiped by both kandas, who is in the form of karma and in the form of Brahma, who is in the form of heaven and in the form of *moksha*. *Yagneshā*! *Achyutā*! *Govindā*! *Mādavā*! *Anantā*! *Keshavā*! *Krishnā*! *Vishnu*! *Hrishikeshā*! *Vāsudevā*! Salutations to you".

Lebakaryam

Only if *Anna* (rice) Homam is performed, Lebakaryam should be performed – Place the big *dharvi* on the right side of the ghee bowl and the small *dharvi* in the middle. Take the *darbais* kept under the vessels, touch the big dharvi with the tip, the small dharvi in the middle and the ghee bowl with bottom – likewise three times. Keeping one *darbai* in the lap and the others, should be added to Agni. Again, touch the water and add the *darbai* kept in the lap to the fire. Point three fingers and chant Agni *Abhimantram* and touch the earth.

समर्पणम् ॥

कायेन वाचा मनसेन्द्रियैर्वा बुद्ध्यात्मना वा प्रकृतेः स्वभावात् ।
करोमि यद्यत् सकलं परस्मै नारायणायेति समर्पयामि ॥ १९ ॥

मन्त्रहीनं क्रियाहीनं .....
अभिवादये ..... नमस्कारः ॥

With deficiency, in chanting the *Mantras*, doing the *Kriyas*, without *Bhakti*, whatever Homam was performed by me should be made perfect. Be it prayer, penance, blackness, whatever, the head is best, if you think of Sri Krishna.

Whatever I do with my body, speech, mind, *Karma* organs, *Gnana* organs, or the movement of nature, I submit everything to the Lord *Narayana*.

Abhivādaye ..... Namaskāraḥ ||

रक्षा । बृहत् साम क्षत्रभृद्वृद्धवृष्णियं त्रिष्टुभौजश्शुभित-
मुग्रवीरम् । इन्द्र स्तोमेन पञ्चदशेन मध्यमिदं वातेन सगरेण रक्ष ॥१८॥

May the *Bruhatsama Mantra*, which preserves strength, develops virility, bestows *dharana* energy and supreme welfare, warrior sons, in the form of Drushtup Chandas, protect us. Lord Indra! Wait for this body that appears between the two periods.

Take some *darba*, flower, *akshatai* and water and surround the fire saying "*Idanīm Agnim Āvāhita Samasta Devatām, Kumbe Arpayāmi*" and add all the deities who have been in the Agni so far, to the *kumbha*.

Then complete the Pooja again to the deities in the Kumbha. Do not perform *Yatāsthanam* to the deities in the Kumbha if *abhishekam* of the Kumbha water is to be done to the idols of other deities. To perform *abhishekam* for human beings, *Yatāsthanam* to the deities in the Kumbha need to be done.

*****

***Vaidhīkam* or *Tāntrīkam*?**

We have earlier seen that Chandee Homam can be done according to Vedic or Tantric methods. What is the difference between these two? Let us take a look at which can be used when and by whom.

It is Vedic to do according to the methods prescribed by the Veda scriptures. Doing according to the methods prescribed by the Tantric texts is Tantric. We all know the Veda scriptures to some extent. What are tantric texts? We have not heard much!

The term 'Tantric' is based on a comment by Kulluka Bhatta on Manava Dharma sastra 2.1, who contrasted Vaidik and Tantric forms of Shruti. The Tantric, is that literature which forms a parallel part of the Hindu tradition, independent of the Vedic corpus. The Vedic and non-Vedic (Tantric) paths are seen as two different approaches to ultimate reality, the Vedic approach based on Brahman and Tantric being based on the non-Vedic Agama texts. Despite Bhatta attempt to clarify, in reality Hindus and Buddhists have historically felt free to borrow and blend ideas from all sources, Vedic, non-Vedic and in the case of Buddhism, its own canonical works. Trika or Kashmir Shaivism may also be referred to as Tantric.

One of the key differences between the Tantric and non-Tantric traditions – whether it be orthodox Buddhism, Hinduism or Jainism – is their assumptions about the need for monastic or ascetic life. Non-Tantric, or orthodox traditions in all three major ancient Indian religions, hold that the worldly life of a householder is one driven by desires and greeds which are a serious impediment to spiritual liberation (moksha, nirvana, kaivalya). These orthodox traditions teach renunciation of householder life, a mendicant's life of simplicity and leaving all attachments to become a monk or nun. In contrast, the Tantric traditions hold, that "both enlightenment and worldly success" are achievable and that "this world need not be shunned to achieve enlightenment". Yet, even this supposed categorical divergence is debatable, e.g., Bhagavad Gita (2:48-53) says, including "Yoga is skill in [the performance of] actions".

Tantra is an individuated practice for realizing unity consciousness, whereas Vedic Yagnas are meant to scale this to all of society because it is very difficult to perform Tantric practices in modern society.

Tantras are derived from Agamas and are usually a subset. There are many agamas that are again classified into Shaiva agama, Shakta agamas,

Vaishnava agama (e.g., Pancharatra texts). A tantric scripture usually has the knowledge relevant to yantras, mantras, the rituals and techniques employed in the worship of a deity. Like the Vedic tradition, even the tantric wisdom is passed down from a master to disciple.

There is one peculiar thing about Tantra – The wisdom of the tantras is so distilled that it is possible for its application to fall out of line with the true spirit of Vedas, especially when other aspects of Shruti such as dharma and karma are ignored. This is why some practices from the tantras are considered *avaideeka*. For example – Sat karma prayogas and such practices mentioned in tantras can be used by people to protect dharma. They completely destroy the one who resorts to such practices when employed without considering Desha, kala, karma and dharma.

It is also dangerous for someone to simply pick up the tantra. It is like walking on the knife's edge. If deviated a little may end-up with evil results. We all have heard of *Taantreeka/ Maantreeka* mostly prevalent in Kerala – so shown in movies.

Hence, it can be derived that Vaidheeka method can be followed by those who have studied Vedas and Tantric method by others.

Earlier days Brahmins, Kshatriyas and Vyshyas got Brahmopadesa and were wearing yagnopaveeda. They also learnt Vedas. But nowadays, this has been diluted and only Brahmins get Brahmopadesa, wear yagnopaveedas and learn Vedas. Resultantly, only those whose have learnt Vedas are eligible to follow Vaidheeka methods.

On the other hand, everyone irrespective of caste/ creed/ religion/ sex can chant Devi Maahaatmyam. The only prescription is having got initiated in Navaaksharee Japam by an appropriate guru. They can also perform Chandi homam. However, some other restrictions are prescribed to perform Chandi homam – Brahmacharis, widowers, ladies, whose wives are out of doors or pregnant are not eligible to perform Chandi homam.

Hence, those who have not learnt Vedas, can perform Chandi Homam only through Tantric method. Others can perform any one method either Vedic or Tantric.

Further other *mantras* are based on *Vedas* and hence those *homams* are done using *Vaidheeka* methods. But Sri Devi Mahatmyam is from Purana and not based on Vedas. Hence, its homam has to be done using Tantric methods only.

Also, all the Shakta related texts are called as Tantra texts. Devi Mahaatmyam or Chandi is very well listed in this Tantra Text group and hence it is all the more apt to perform Chandi homam through Tantric method.

*****

Caṇḍī Homam

Śrī Devī Māhātmyam – this literally means praising *Śrī Devī*. This text has 700 verses and hence it is also called as *Saptaśatī* (*Sapta* = 7, *śatam* = 100). It is also called as "*Durgā Saptaśatī*". This is read in the midst of "*Mārkaṇḍeya Purāṇam*". Hence it is concluded that sage *Mārkaṇḍeya* is the author of this text. However, all the *Purāṇas* were written by Sage *Veda Vyāsa* and hence he should be author of this also.

Caṇḍī havan (*homa*) is perfomed with these verses only. Hence, this is called as '*Caṇḍī*' itself. As a part of chanting this *Caṇḍi* some other verses are also chant as a prelude and/ or suffixing. They are given below in the order of chanting;

- श्री सिद्ध कुञ्जिका स्तोत्रम्
- श्री देव्या: कवचम्
- श्री अर्गला स्तोत्रम्
- श्री कीलक स्तोत्रम्
- वेदोक्त रात्रि सूक्तम्
- नवाक्षरी मन्त्र:
- सप्तशती न्यास:
- श्री देवी माहात्म्यम् – all the 13 chapters. There are some variance among the diffirent publishings. Again we are not into the argument of which is correct and which is wrong. We follow the one taught by our *gurus*. Those who are not able to chant all the *13* chapters in one go can read only the middle charitram. All the *13* chapters can be chant continously for 7 days in this order - 1; 2-3; 4; 5-6-7-8; 9-10; 11; & 12-13.
- प्राधानिक रहस्यम्
- वैकृति रहस्यम्
- मूर्ति रहस्यम्
- श्री देवी सूक्तम्
- श्री दुर्गा सूक्तम्
- क्षमा प्रार्थना

- देव्यपराधा क्षमापन स्तोत्रम्

This Sri Devi Mahatmya narrates the story of Chandika Parameshwari, the combined form of Maha Kali, Maha Lakshmi and Maha Saraswati, by Sumedha Maharishi, to a king named Surathan and a Vaishya named Samathi. It consists of 13 chapters as seen below;

The first story pertaining to Maha Kali;

1. The slaying of the demons Madhu-Kaidapa.

Middle story pertaining to Maha Lakshmi;

2. Destroying the entire army of Mahishasura
3. Slaying of the demon Mahishasura
4. Praising by Devas

The last story pertaining to Maha Saraswati;

5. Dialogue between Sri Devi and the Messenger Sugreevan.
6. Slaying of the demon Dhoomralochanan
7. Slaying of demons Chanda-Munda
8. Slaying of the demon Raktabeejan
9. Slaying of the demon Nishumban
10. Slaying of the demon Shumban
11. Praising Sri Devi
12. Phala Shruti – Results
13. Vara Pradhanam – showring boons

Thus, the story of Sri Devi slaying the demons such as Madhu-Kaitabas, Mahishasura, Dhoomralochana, Chanda-Mundas, Raktabeejan and Shumba-Nishumba has been narrated in detail in this text.

After the Kurukshetra battle in the Maha Bharata, the Pandavas ruled the integrated part Hastinapuram and Indraprastam. After them, Arjuna's son Abhimanyu's son Parikshit came to power. He too was bitten by a snake named Dakshagan due to the curse of a son of a sage and died. On the verge of death, Sri Vishnu Bhagavatam was recited for 7 days (Saptaham) by Shuka Maharishi, son of Veda Vyasa and became blessed.

After that Parikshit's son Janamejayan reigned. He, after his father was bitten by a snake, vowed to eradicate the Naga dynasty from the world and began performing the "Sarpa Yaga". Bunch of Nagas fell into that holy fire and started dying. Janamejayan stopped the yagna at the request of Indra.

The Pandavas and Kauravas were afflicted with Brahma-Hatti dosha as they killed many in war. Parikshit too was bitten by a snake and died untimely. Thus, Janamejaya's ancestors suffered without attaining salvation. Hence, Veda Vyasa narrated "Sri Devi Bhagavata" for 9 days (Navaham) to Janamejaya. Then he made him perform Chandi Homam. Through this all his ancestors attained salvation. This is the first record about Chandi Homam.

Chandee Homa is being performed in various ways depending on available time and wealth as below;

- Nava Chandi – 9 times Parayanam and 9 times Homam.
- Shata Chandi – 100 times Parayanam and 10 times Homam.
- Sahasra Chandi – 1,000 times Parayanam and 100 times Homam.
- Ayuda Chandi – 10,000 times recitation and 1,000 times homam.

During Chandi Homam, it is customary to perform a Poornahuti at the end of each chapter and Maha Poornahuti at the end. They add as much materials as they can to the Poornahuti. Effort and devotion are more important than quantity and calculation of dravyams. At the time of Maha Poornahuti, some recite *Bhavanopanishat*[7]. A sample *poornahuti* items is shown in the picture.

[7] Detailed in a separate chapter.

Sacrifices (bali) are offered to 64 Yoginis Sahita Bhairavas as part of Chandi Homam. A live sample of *bali* is shown in the picture.

As part of this, Dampati, Sumangali, Vadu (Brahmachari) and Kanya Pujas are also performed.

Doing this yagya will bring worldly benefits. The fear of the enemy will disappear. Goddess Lakshmi will shower her blessings. Improvement in children's education, unmarried people can get married. The child-less will be blessed with a child. Career advancement, success in all things. It is said in the Chandi Mantra itself that all kinds of sins and diseases will be cured if anyone listens to the mantras while performing this, Yagya.

Glory and Benefits of Candi Yagna

According to the phrase "*Deivādīnam Jagatsraşţam Mantrādīnam tu Daivatam*" – all creations are under the control of the deity. All the deities, who are the cause of the world are possessed by *mantras*. Such *Mahamantras* have been given to us by our forefathers, *Maharishis* who practiced penance and learned them through their *Divya Drushti* (divine sight). *Yantra*, *mantra* and *moorti* (idol) should all come together, if there is to be sanctity of the deity. From this, we can clearly understand the glory of the *mantras*.

Lord Krishna preached, Srimad Bhagavad Gita, to Arjuna, which is seen in the middle of Maha Bharata. It consists of 700 verses. It holds within itself the *Adyatma Vidyai*. Similarly, "Sri Devi Mahatmyam", which is seen, in the middle of Markandeya Purana also has 700 shlokas. It is popularly known as *'Candee'* since it glorifies Goddess Chandika and as 'Saptasathee' as it has 700 shlokas. Karmayogam, Bhaktiyogam and Jnanayogam are preached in Sri Devi Mahatmyam also as in Srimad Bhagavad Gita. That is why Sri Devi Mahatmyam is hailed as "Shākta Gita".

Sri Devi Mahatmyam consists of 3 sections, 13 chapters and 700 verses. These three sections tell the story of the three Shaktis viz., Mahakali, Mahalakshmi and Mahasaraswati. These three are the essences of Rigveda, Yajurveda and Samaveda respectively. These three include the *'Aim'*, the *Vāgbhava Beejam* called, *'Hreem'* the *Māya* (or Bhuvaneshwari) *Beejam* and the *Kāma Beejam* called *'Kleem'* respectively. Srimad Bhagavad Gita was preached by Lord Krishna to all the people of the world keeping Arjuna as a cause. Similarly, the treasure of the three Shaktis, Sri Devi Mahatmyam, which was advised to all the people by the Sage Sumedhas, to the King Suratan and the business man *Samathi.*

Although Sri Devi Mahatmyam may superficially appear to tell the story of destroying the demons, its ultimate goal is to save the world. It is impossible to fully describe the benefits of doing Chandi Homam or chanting the same. In Rahasyatrayam "*Jagan Māta: Candikāya: Keerthitā: Kamadenava:*" – one who chants or performs homam the glories of Jaganmata Chandikadevi all his desires will be fulfilled like Kamadenu.

According to the saying "*Kalau Candī Vināyakau*", in this *Kaliyuga*, worshiping Lord Vinayaka and Goddess *Candee* is easy, simple and can give all sorts of benefits. In the 12th chapter of Sri Devi Mahatmya, Mother Parashakti bestows many boons by her very words. Those who worship the Mother and have darshan with devotion will get rid of all the sufferings and increase in wealth. There is no doubt about it. Great victory in war and bad dreams will go away.

Terrible bodily and mental sorrows will be removed and all the planets will bless. Children will get rid of *Balarishtam*, a childhood disease and will get health. Enmities caused by fate in the family will be removed and love will prevail. The separated will come together. Evil forces such as witchcraft, sorcery, voodooisam, etc., caused by enemies will be removed and good will be achieved. Sufferings caused by deadly forest fires and poisonous animals will be removed. All the miseries caused by natural calamities such as storms, floods, tsunamis, earthquakes, famines due to lack of rain and all will be removed and people will benefit.

If one chants, hears and even thinks the name *'Durge'*, the Mother will save him, just as a small boat comes to save a drowning person in the sea.

As a summary, *Mangala Candi Homam* is capable of bestowing all wealth to mankind. May Sri Devi bless everyone to get all the benefits.

*****

Śrī Caṇḍī Prātaḥ Smaraṇam

Prātaḥ Smarāmi Śaradindukarojjvalābhāṃ
Sadratnavanmakarakuṇḍalahārabhūṣām ।
Divyāyudhorjitasunīlasahasrahastāṃ
Raktotpalābhacaraṇāṃ Mahatīṃ Pareśām ॥ 1

Prātarnamāmi Mahiṣāsuracaṇḍamuṇḍa-
Śumbhāsuraprasukhadaityavināśadakṣām ।
Brahmendramunimohanaśīlalīlāṃ
Caṇḍīṃ Samastasuramūrtimanekarūpām ॥ 2

Prātarbhajāmi Bhavatāmabhilāṣadātrīṃ Bhajatamabhilasha
Dhātrīṃ Samastajagatāṃ Duritāpahantrīm ।
Saṃsārabandhanavimocanahetubhūtāṃ
Māyāṃ Parāṃ Samadhigamya Parasya Viṣṇoḥ ॥ 3

Ślokatrayamidaṃ Devyāścaṇḍikāyāḥ Paṭhennaraḥ ।
Sarvānkāmānavāpnoti Viṣṇuloke Mahīyate ॥ 4

Iti Śrī Caṇḍī Prātaḥ Smaraṇaṃ Sampūrṇam ।

श्री चण्डी प्रातः स्मरणम्

प्रातः स्मरामि शरदिन्दुकरोज्ज्वलाभां सद्रत्नवन्मकरकुण्डलहारभूषाम् ।
दिव्यायुधोर्जितसुनीलसहस्रहस्तां रक्तोत्पलाभचरणां महतीं परेशाम् ॥ १

प्रातर्नमामि महिषासुरचण्डमुण्ड-शुम्भासुरप्रसुखदैत्यविनाशदक्षाम् ।
ब्रह्मेन्द्रमुनिमोहनशीललीलां चण्डीं समस्तसुरमूर्तिमनेकरूपाम् ॥ २

प्रातर्भजामि भवतामभिलाषदात्रीं धात्रीं समस्तजगतां दुरितापहन्त्रीम् ।
संसारबन्धनविमोचनहेतुभूतां मायां परां समधिगम्य परस्य विष्णोः ॥ ३

श्लोकत्रयमिदं देव्याश्चण्डिकायाः पठेन्नरः ।
सर्वान्कामानवाप्नोति विष्णुलोके महीयते ॥ ४

इति श्री चण्डी प्रातः स्मरणं सम्पूर्णम् ।

*****

Śrī Caṇḍī Pāṭhaḥ

The numbering for verses are from the 5th chapter of the book Chandi, in which the Devas were singing this particular stava as they were ousted by the demons, Shumbha and Nishumbha from Devaloka. The numbers are verse numbers, each Namastasyai is for one of the triple manifestations described in one word, for example Vishnumaya is three;

Sāttvik, *Rājasik* and *Tāmasik*

and the *namo namaḥ* is also three;

Kāyik, Vāchik and Mānasik I

II *Oṃ Śrī Devyai Namaḥ* II

Yā Devī Sarvabhūteṣu Viṣṇumāyeti Śabditā I

Namastasyai 14 *Namastasyai* 15 *Namastasyai Namo Namaḥ* II 5-16

Yā Devī Sarvabhūteṣu Cetanetyabhidhīyate I

Namastasyai 17 *Namastasyai* 18 *Namastasyai Namo Namaḥ* II 5-19

Yā Devī Sarvabhūteṣu Buddhirūpeṇa Saṃsthitā I

Namastasyai 20 *Namastasyai* 21 *Namastasyai Namo Namaḥ* II 5-22

Yā Devī Sarvabhūteṣu Nidrārūpeṇa Saṃsthitā I

Namastasyai 23 *Namastasyai* 24 *Namastasyai Namo Namaḥ* II 5-25

Yā Devī Sarvabhūteṣu Kṣudhārūpeṇa Saṃsthitā I

Namastasyai 26 *Namastasyai* 27 *Namastasyai Namo Namaḥ* II 5-28

Yā Devī Sarvabhūteṣu Cchāyārūpeṇa Saṃsthitā I

Namastasyai 29 *Namastasyai* 30 *Namastasyai Namo Namaḥ* II 5-31

Yā Devī Sarvabhūteṣu Śaktirūpeṇa Saṃsthitā I

Namastasyai 32 *Namastasyai* 33 *Namastasyai Namo Namaḥ* II 5-34

Yā Devī Sarvabhūteṣu Tṛṣṇārūpeṇa Saṃsthitā I

Namastasyai 35 *Namastasyai* 36 *Namastasyai Namo Namaḥ* II 5-37

Yā Devī Sarvabhūteṣu Kṣāntirūpeṇa Saṃsthitā I

Namastasyai 38 *Namastasyai* 39 *Namastasyai Namo Namaḥ* II 5-40

Yā Devī Sarvabhūteṣu Jātirūpeṇa Saṃsthitā I

Namastasyai 41 *Namastasyai* 42 *Namastasyai Namo Namaḥ* II 5-43

Yā Devī Sarvabhūteṣu Lajjārūpeṇa Saṃsthitā I

Namastasyai 44 *Namastasyai* 45 *Namastasyai Namo Namaḥ* II 5-46

Yā Devī Sarvabhūteṣu Śāntirūpeṇa Saṃsthitā I

Namastasyai 47 *Namastasyai* 48 *Namastasyai Namo Namaḥ* II 5-49

Yā Devī Sarvabhūteṣu Śraddhārūpeṇa Saṃsthitā I

Namastasyai 50 *Namastasyai* 51 *Namastasyai Namo Namaḥ* II 5-52

Yā Devī Sarvabhūteṣu Kāntirūpeṇa Saṃsthitā I

Namastasyai 53 *Namastasyai* 54 *Namastasyai Namo Namaḥ* II 5-55

Yā Devī Sarvabhūteṣu Lakṣmīrūpeṇa Saṃsthitā I

Namastasyai 56 *Namastasyai* 57 *Namastasyai Namo Namaḥ* II 5-58

Yā Devī Sarvabhūteṣu Vṛttirūpeṇa Saṃsthitā I

Namastasyai 59 *Namastasyai* 60 *Namastasyai Namo Namaḥ* II 5-61

Yā Devī Sarvabhūteṣu Smṛtirūpeṇa Saṃsthitā I

Namastasyai 62 *Namastasyai* 63 *Namastasyai Namo Namaḥ* II 5-64

Yā Devī Sarvabhūteṣu Dayārūpeṇa Saṃsthitā I

Namastasyai 65 *Namastasyai* 66 *Namastasyai Namo Namaḥ* II 5-67

Yā Devī Sarvabhūteṣu Tuṣṭirūpeṇa Saṃsthitā I

Namastasyai 68 *Namastasyai* 69 *Namastasyai Namo Namaḥ* II 5-70

Yā Devī Sarvabhūteṣu Mātṛrūpeṇa Saṃsthitā I

Namastasyai 71 *Namastasyai* 72 *Namastasyai Namo Namaḥ* II 5-73

Yā Devī Sarvabhūteṣu Bhrāntirūpeṇa Saṃsthitā I

Namastasyai 74 *Namastasyai* 75 *Namastasyai Namo Namaḥ* II 5-76

Indriyāṇāmadhiṣṭhātrī Bhutānāñcākhileṣu Yā I

Bhūteṣu Satataṃ Tasyai Vyāptidevyai Namo Namaḥ II 5-77

Citirūpeṇa Yā Kṛtsnametad Vyāpya Sthitā Jagat ।
Namastasyai 78 *Namastasyai* 79 *Namastasyai Namo Namaḥ* ॥ 5-80

॥ *Iti Śrī Caṇḍī Pāṭhaḥ* ॥

श्री चण्डी पाठः

॥ ॐ श्री देव्यै नमः ॥

या देवी सर्वभूतेषु विष्णुमायेति शब्दिता ।
नमस्तस्यै १४ नमस्तस्यै १५ नमस्तस्यै नमो नमः ॥ ५-१६

या देवी सर्वभूतेषु चेतनेत्यभिधीयते ।
नमस्तस्यै १७ नमस्तस्यै १८ नमस्तस्यै नमो नमः ॥ ५-१९

या देवी सर्वभूतेषु बुद्धिरूपेण संस्थिता ।
नमस्तस्यै २० नमस्तस्यै २१ नमस्तस्यै नमो नमः ॥ ५-२२

या देवी सर्वभूतेषु निद्रारूपेण संस्थिता ।
नमस्तस्यै २३ नमस्तस्यै २४ नमस्तस्यै नमो नमः ॥ ५-२५

या देवी सर्वभूतेषु क्षुधारूपेण संस्थिता ।
नमस्तस्यै २६ नमस्तस्यै २७ नमस्तस्यै नमो नमः ॥ ५-२८

या देवी सर्वभूतेषु च्छायारूपेण संस्थिता ।
नमस्तस्यै २९ नमस्तस्यै ३० नमस्तस्यै नमो नमः ॥ ५-३१

या देवी सर्वभूतेषु शक्तिरूपेण संस्थिता ।
नमस्तस्यै ३२ नमस्तस्यै ३३ नमस्तस्यै नमो नमः ॥ ५-३४

या देवी सर्वभूतेषु तृष्णारूपेण संस्थिता ।
नमस्तस्यै ३५ नमस्तस्यै ३६ नमस्तस्यै नमो नमः ॥ ५-३७

या देवी सर्वभूतेषु क्षान्तिरूपेण संस्थिता ।
नमस्तस्यै ३८ नमस्तस्यै ३९ नमस्तस्यै नमो नमः ॥ ५-४०

या देवी सर्वभूतेषु जातिरूपेण संस्थिता ।
नमस्तस्यै ४१ नमस्तस्यै ४२ नमस्तस्यै नमो नमः ॥ ५-४३

या देवी सर्वभूतेषु लज्जारूपेण संस्थिता ।
नमस्तस्यै ४४ नमस्तस्यै ४५ नमस्तस्यै नमो नमः ॥ ५-४६

या देवी सर्वभूतेषु शान्तिरूपेण संस्थिता ।
नमस्तस्यै ४७ नमस्तस्यै ४८ नमस्तस्यै नमो नमः ॥ ५-४९

या देवी सर्वभूतेषु श्रद्धारूपेण संस्थिता ।
नमस्तस्यै ५० नमस्तस्यै ५१ नमस्तस्यै नमो नमः ॥ ५-५२

या देवी सर्वभूतेषु कान्तिरूपेण संस्थिता ।
नमस्तस्यै ५३ नमस्तस्यै ५४ नमस्तस्यै नमो नमः ॥ ५-५५

या देवी सर्वभूतेषु लक्ष्मीरूपेण संस्थिता ।
नमस्तस्यै ५६ नमस्तस्यै ५७ नमस्तस्यै नमो नमः ॥ ५-५८

या देवी सर्वभूतेषु वृत्तिरूपेण संस्थिता ।
नमस्तस्यै ५९ नमस्तस्यै ६० नमस्तस्यै नमो नमः ॥ ५-६१

या देवी सर्वभूतेषु स्मृतिरूपेण संस्थिता ।
नमस्तस्यै ६२ नमस्तस्यै ६३ नमस्तस्यै नमो नमः ॥ ५-६४

या देवी सर्वभूतेषु दयारूपेण संस्थिता ।
नमस्तस्यै ६५ नमस्तस्यै ६६ नमस्तस्यै नमो नमः ॥ ५-६७

या देवी सर्वभूतेषु तुष्टिरूपेण संस्थिता ।
नमस्तस्यै ६८ नमस्तस्यै ६९ नमस्तस्यै नमो नमः ॥ ५-७०

या देवी सर्वभूतेषु मातृरूपेण संस्थिता ।
नमस्तस्यै ७१ नमस्तस्यै ७२ नमस्तस्यै नमो नमः ॥ ५-७३

या देवी सर्वभूतेषु भ्रान्तिरूपेण संस्थिता ।
नमस्तस्यै ७४ नमस्तस्यै ७५ नमस्तस्यै नमो नमः ॥ ५-७६

इन्द्रियाणामधिष्ठात्री भुतानाञ्चाखिलेषु या ।
भूतेषु सततं तस्यै व्याप्तिदेव्यै नमो नमः ॥ ५-७७

चितिरूपेण या कृत्स्नमेतद् व्याप्य स्थिता जगत् ।
नमस्तस्यै ७८ नमस्तस्यै ७९ नमस्तस्यै नमो नमः ॥ ५-८०

॥ इति श्री चंडी पाठः ॥

*****

Śrī Caṇḍikā Hṛdaya Stotram

Asya Śrī Caṇḍikā Hṛdaya Stotra Mahāmantrasya |

Mārkkaṇḍeya Ṛṣiḥ, Anuṣṭupcchandaḥ, Śrī Caṇḍikā Devatā |
Hrāṃ Bījaṃ, Hrīṃ Śaktiḥ, Hrūṃ Kīlakaṃ,
Śrī Caṇḍikā Prasāda Siddhyarthe Jape Viniyogaḥ |

Hrāṃ Ityādi Ṣaḍaṃga Nyāsaḥ |

Dhyānaṃ |

Sarvamaṃgaḷa Māṃgalye Śive Sarvārttha Sādhike |
Śaraṇye Tryambake Gaurī Nārāyaṇī Namo'stute ||

Brahmovāca |

Athātassaṃ Pravakṣyāmi Vistareṇa Yathātathaṃ |
Caṇḍikā Hṛdayaṃ Guhyaṃ Śṛṇuṣvaikāgramānasaḥ ||

Oṃ Aiṃ Hrīṃ Kḷīṃ, Hrāṃ, Hrīṃ, Hrūṃ Jaya Jaya Cāmuṇḍe, Caṇḍike, Tridaśa, Maṇimakuṭakoṭīra Saṃghaṭṭita Caraṇāravinde, Gāyatrī, Sāvitrī, Sarasvati, Mahāhikṛtābharaṇe, Bhairavarūpa Dhāriṇī, Prakaṭita Daṃṣṭrogravadane,Ghore, Ghorānanejvala

Jvalajjvālā Sahasraparivṛte, Mahāṭṭahāsa Badharīkṛta Digantare, Sarvāyudha Paripūrṇṇe, Kapālahaste, Gajājinottarīye, Bhūtavetāḷabṛndaparivṛte, Prakanpita Dharādhare, Madhukaiṭamahiṣāsura, Dhūmralocana Caṇḍamuṇḍaraktabīja

Śuṃbhaniśuṃbhādi Daityaniṣkaṇḍhake, Kāḷarātri, Mahāmāye, Śive, Nitye, Indrāgniyamanirṛti Varuṇavāyu Someśāna Pradhāna Śakti Bhūte, Brahmāviṣṇu Śivastute, Tribhuvanādhārādhāre, Vāme, Jyeṣṭhe, Raudryaṃbike,

Brāhmī, Māheśvari, Kaumāri, Vaiṣṇavī Śaṃkhinī Vārāhīndrāṇī Cāmuṇḍā Śivadūti Mahākāḷi Mahālakṣmī, Mahāsarasvatītisthite, Nādamadhyasthite, Mahograviṣoragaphaṇāmaṇighaṭita Makuṭakaṭakādiratna Mahājvālāmaya Pādabāhudaṇḍottamāṃge,

Mahāmahiṣopari Gandharva Vidyādharārādhite,
Navaratnanidhikośe Tattvasvarūpe Vākpāṇipādapāyūpasthātmike,
Śabdasparśarūparasagandhādi Svarūpe,
Tvakcakṣuḥ Śrotrajihvāghrāṇamahābuddhisthite,

Oṃ Aiṃkāra Hrīṃ Kāra Kḷīṃ Kārahaste Āṃ Kroṃ Āgneyanayanapātre Praveśaya, Drāṃ Śoṣaya Śoṣaya, Drīṃ Sukumāraya Sukumāraya, Śrīṃ Sarvaṃ Praveśaya Praveśaya, Trailokyavara Varṇṇini Samasta Cittaṃ Vaśīkaru Vaśīkaru Mama Śatrūn,

Śīghraṃ Māraya Māraya, Jāgrat Svapna Suṣuptya Vasthāsu Asmān Rājacorāgnijala Vāta Viṣabhūta-Śatrumṛtyu-Jvarādi Sphoṭakādi Nānārogebhyoḥ Nānābhicārebhyo Nānāpavādebhyaḥ Parakarma Mantra Tantra Yantrauṣadha Śalyaśūnya Kṣudrebhyaḥ Samyaṅmāṃ

Rakṣa Rakṣa, Oṃ Aiṃ Hrāṃ Hrīṃ Hrūṃ Hraiṃ Hraḥ, Sphrāṃ Sphrīṃ Sphraiṃ Sphrauṃ Sphraḥ - Mama Sarva Kāryāṇi Sādhaya Sādhaya Huṃ Phaṭ Svāhā - Rāja Dvāre Śmaśāne Vā Vivāde Śatru Saṅkaṭe । Bhūtāgni Cora Maddhyasthe Mayi Kāryāṇi Sādhaya ॥ Svāhā ।

Caṇḍikā Hṛdayaṃ Guhyaṃ Trisandhyaṃ Yaḥ Paṭhennaraḥ ।
Sarva Kāma Pradaṃ Puṃsāṃ Bhukti Muktiṃ Priyaccati ॥

॥ *Iti Śrī Caṇḍikā Hṛdaya Stotram Sampūrṇam* ॥

श्री चण्डिका हृदय स्तोत्रम्

अस्य श्री चण्डिका हृदय स्तोत्र महामन्त्रस्य ।
मार्क्कण्डेय ऋषिः, अनुष्टुप्च्छन्दः, श्री चण्डिका देवता ।
ह्रां बीजं, ह्रीं शक्तिः, ह्रूं कीलकं,
श्री चण्डिका प्रसाद सिद्ध्यर्थे जपे विनियोगः ।
ह्रां इत्यादि षडंग न्यासः ।

ध्यानं ।

सर्वमंगळ मांगल्ये शिवे सर्वार्त्थ साधिके ।
शरण्ये त्र्यम्बके गौरी नारायणी नमोऽस्तुते ॥

ब्रह्मोवाच ।

अथातस्सं प्रवक्ष्यामि विस्तरेण यथातथं ।
चण्डिका हृदयं गुह्यं शृणुष्वैकाग्रमानसः ॥

ॐ ऐं ह्रीं क्ळीं, ह्रां, ह्रीं, ह्रूं जय जय चामुण्डे,
चण्डिके, त्रिदश, मणिमकुटकोटीर संघट्टित चरणारविन्दे,
गायत्री, सावित्री, सरस्वति, महाहिकृताभरणे, भैरवरूप
धारिणी, प्रकटित दंष्ट्रोग्रवदने,घोरे, घोराननेज्वल

ज्वलज्ज्वाला सहस्रपरिवृते, महाट्टहास बधरीकृत दिगन्तरे,
सर्वायुध परिपूर्णे, कपालहस्ते, गजाजिनोत्तरीये,
भूतवेताळबृन्दपरिवृते, प्रकन्पित धराधरे,
मधुकैटमहिषासुर, धूम्रलोचन चण्डमुण्डरक्तबीज

शुंभनिशुंभादि दैत्यनिष्कण्ढके, काळरात्रि,
महामाये, शिवे, नित्ये, इन्द्राग्नियमनिरृति वरुणवायु
सोमेशान प्रधान शक्ति भूते, ब्रह्माविष्णु शिवस्तुते,
त्रिभुवनाधाराधारे, वामे, ज्येष्ठे, रौद्र्यंबिके,

ब्राह्मी, माहेश्वरि, कौमारि, वैष्णवी शंखिनी वाराहीन्द्राणी
चामुण्डा शिवदूति महाकाळि महालक्ष्मी, महासरस्वतीतिस्थिते,
नादमध्यस्थिते, महोग्रविषोरगफणामणिघटित
मकुटकटकादिरत्न महाज्वालामय पादबाहुदण्डोत्तमांगे,

महामहिषोपरि गन्धर्व विद्याधराराधिते,
नवरत्ननिधिकोशे तत्त्वस्वरूपे वाक्पाणिपादपायूपस्थात्मिके,
शब्दस्पर्शरूपरसगन्धादि स्वरूपे, त्वक्चक्षुः श्रोत्रजिह्वाघ्राणमहाबुद्धिस्थिते,

ॐ ऐंकार ह्रीं कार क्ळीं कारहस्ते आं क्रों आग्नेयनयनपात्रे प्रवेशय,
द्रां शोषय शोषय, द्रीं सुकुमारय सुकुमारय,
श्रीं सर्वं प्रवेशय प्रवेशय, त्रैलोक्यवर वर्णिनि
समस्त चित्तं वशीकरु वशीकरु मम शत्रून्,

शीघ्रं मारय मारय, जाग्रत् स्वप्न सुषुप्त्य वस्थासु अस्मान्
राजचोराग्निजल वात विषभूत-शत्रुमृत्यु-ज्वरादि स्फोटकादि
नानारोगेभ्योः नानाभिचारेभ्यो नानापवादेभ्यः परकर्म मन्त्र

तन्त्र यन्त्रौषध शल्यशून्य क्षुद्रेभ्यः सम्यङ्गां
रक्ष रक्ष, ॐ ऐं ह्रां ह्रीं ह्रूं ह्रैं ह्रः,
स्फ्रां स्फ्रीं स्फ्रैं स्फ्रौं स्फ्रः - मम सर्व कार्याणि
साधय साधय हुं फट् स्वाहा -राज द्वारे श्मशाने वा विवादे शत्रु सङ्कटे ।

भूताग्नि चोर मद्ध्यस्थे मयि कार्याणि साधय ॥ स्वाहा ।

चण्डिका हृदयं गुह्यं त्रिसन्ध्यं यः पठेन्नरः ।
सर्व काम प्रदं पुंसां भुक्ति मुक्तिं प्रियच्चति ॥

॥ इति श्री चण्डिका हृदय स्तोत्रम् सम्पूर्णम् ॥

*****

Bhāvanopaniṣat

This belongs to *Atharva Veda*. This is normally chant during *Pūrnāhuti* of *Candī Homa*-s. In some schools this is also called as *Śrīcakropaniṣat*. Still, there is one other *Upaniṣat* called, *Śrīcakropaniṣat*.

Svāvidyāpadatatkāryaṃ Śrīcakropari Bhāsuram ।

Bindurūpaśivākāraṃ Rāmacandrapadaṃ Bhaje ॥

Śānti Mantraḥ ।

Oṃ Bhadraṃ Karṇebhiḥ Śṛṇuyāma Devāḥ ॥

Bhadraṃ Paśyemākṣabhiryajatrāḥ ॥

Sthirairaṅgaistuṣṭuvāġ̃ Sastanūbhiḥ ॥ *Vyaśema Devahitaṃ Yadāyuḥ* ॥

Svasti Na Indro Vṛddhaśravāḥ ॥ *Svasti Naḥ Pūṣā Viśvavedāḥ* ॥

Svasti Nastārkṣyo Ariṣṭanemiḥ ॥ *Svasti No Bṛhaspatirdadhātu* ॥

Oṃ Śāntiḥ Śāntiḥ Śāntiḥ ॥

Hariḥ Oṃ ।

Ātmānamakhaṇḍamaṇḍalākāramavṛtya Sakalabrahmāṇḍamaṇḍalaṃ Svaprakāśaṃ Dhyāyet । *Oṃ Śrīguruḥ Sarvakāraṇabhūtā Śaktiḥ* ।

Tena Navarandhrarūpo Dehaḥ । *Navaśaktirūpaṃ Śrīcakram* ।

Vārāhī Pitṛrūpā । *Kurukullā Balidevatā Mātā* ।

Puruṣārthāḥ Sāgarāḥ । *Deho Navaratnadvīpaḥ* ।

Tvagādisaptadhātubhiranekaiḥ Saṃyuktāḥ Saṅkalpāḥ Kalpataravaḥ ।

Tejaḥ Kalpakodyānam । *Rasanayā Bhāvyamānā Madhurāmlatiktakaṭukaṣāyalavaṇabhedāḥ Ṣaḍrasāḥ*

Ṣaḍṛtavaḥ Kriyāśaktiḥ Pīṭham । *Kuṇḍalinī Jñānaśaktirgṛham* ।

Icchāśaktirmahātripurasundarī । *Jñātā Hotā Jñānamagniḥ*

(Jñānamarghyam) Jñeyaṃ Haviḥ ।

Jñātṛjñānajñeyānāmabhedabhāvanaṃ Śrīcakrapūjanam ।

Niyatisahitāḥ Śṛṅgārādayo Nava Rasā Aṇimādayaḥ ।

Kāmakrodhalobhamohamadamātsaryapuṇyapāpamayā Brāhmyādyaṣṭaśaktayaḥ । *(Ādharanavakam Mudrāśaktayaḥ* ।*)*

Pṛthivyaptejovāyvākāśaśrotratvakcakṣurjihvāghrāṇavākpāṇipādapāyūpas thamanovikārāḥ (Kāmākarṣiṇyādi) Ṣoḍaṣa Śaktayaḥ |

Vacanādānagamanavisargānandahāno(Pādāno)Pekṣā(Khya)-Bhuddhayo'naṅgakusumādiśaktayo'ṣṭau |

Alambusā Kuhūrviśvodarī Varuṇā Hastijihvā Yaśasvatyaśvinī Gāndhārī Pūṣā Śaṅkhinī Sarasvatīḍā Piṅgalā Suṣumnā Ceti Caturdaśa Nāḍyaḥ |

Sarvasaṃkṣobhiṇyādicaturdaśāragā Devatāḥ |

Prāṇā Pāna Vyāno Dāna Samānanāga Kūrmakṛkara Devadattadhanañjayā Iti Daśa Vāyavaḥ |

Sarvasiddhipradā D,.evyo Bahirdaśāragā Devatāḥ |

Etadvāyudaśakasaṃsargopādhibhedhena Recaka Pūrakaśoṣakadāha Plāvakā (Recakaḥ Pācakaḥ Śoṣako Dāhakaḥ Plāvakā Iti) Prāṇamukhyatvena Pañcadho'sti (Jaṭharāgnirbhavati) |

Kṣārako Dārakaḥ Kṣobhako Mohako Jṛmbhaka Ityapālanamukhyatvena Pañcavidho'sti |

Tena Manuṣyāṇāṃ Mohako Dāhako (Nāgaprādhānyena Pañcabidhāste Manuṣyāṇāṃ Dehagā) Bhakṣyabhojyaśoṣyalehyapeyātmakaṃ Caturvidhamannaṃ (Pañcavidhamannaṃ) Pācayati |

Etā Daśa Vahnikalāḥ Sarvajñatvādyantardaśāragā Devatāḥ |

Śītoṣṇasukhaduḥkhecchāsattvarajastamoguṇā Vaśinyādiśaktayo'ṣṭau |

Śabdasparśarūparasagandhāḥ Pañcatanmātrāḥ Pañcapuṣpabāṇā Mana Ikṣudhanuḥ | Vaśyo Vāṇo Rāgaḥ Pāśaḥ | Dveṣo'ṅkuśaḥ |

Avyaktamahattattvamahadahaṅkāra Iti Kāmeśvarī-Vajreśvarī-Bhagamālinyo'ntastrikoṇāgragā Devatāḥ | (Nirupādhikasaṃvideva Kāmeśvara | Sadānandapūrṇa Svātmeva Paradevatā Lalitā | Lauhityametasya Sarvasya Vimarśa | Ananyacittatvena Ca Siddhiḥ | Bhāvanāyāḥ Kriyā Upacaraḥ | Ahaṃ Tvamasti Nāsti Kartavyamakartavyamupāsitavyamiti Vikalpānāmātmani Vilāpanam Homaḥ | Bhavanāviṣayāṇāmabhedabhavanā Tarpaṇam |)

Pañcadaśatithirūpeṇa Kālasya Pariṇāmāvalokanasthitiḥ Pañcadaśanityāḥ | Śraddhānurūpā Dhīrdevatā |

Tayoḥ Kāmeśvarī Sadānandaghanā Paripūrṇasvātmaikyarūpā Devatā | Salilamiti Lauhityakāraṇaṃ Sattvam |

Kartavyamakartavyamiti Bhāvanāyukta Upacāraḥ ।

Asti Nāstīti Kartavyatānūpacāraḥ ।

Bāhyābhyantaḥkaraṇānāṃ Rūpagrahaṇayogyatāsttvityāvāhanam ।

Tasya Bāhyābhyantaḥkaraṇānāmekarūpaviṣayagrahaṇamāsanam ।

Raktaśuklapadaikīkaraṇaṃ Pādyam ।

Ujjvaladāmodānandāsanadānamarghyam ।

Svacchaṃ Svataḥsiddhamityācamanīyam ।

Ciccandramayīti Sarvāṅgasravaṇaṃ Snānam ।

Cidagnisvarūpaparamānandaśaktisphuraṇaṃ Vastram ।
Pratyekaṃ Saptaviṃśatidhā Bhinna Tvenec Chājñānakriyātmaka
Brahmagranthimadrasatantubrahmanāḍī Brahmasūtram ।

Svavyatiriktavastusaṅgarahitasmaraṇāṃ Vibhūṣaṇam ।

Saccitsukhaparipūrṇatāsmaraṇaṃ Gandhaḥ ।

Samastaviṣayāṇāṃ Manasaḥ Sthairyeṇānusaṃdhānaṃ Kusumam ।

Teṣāmeva Sarvadā Svīkaraṇaṃ Dhūpaḥ ।

Pavanāvacchinnotdhvajvalanasaccidulkākāśadeho Dīpaḥ ।

Samastayātāyātavarjyaṃ Naivedyam ।

Avasthātrayāṇāmekīkaraṇaṃ Tāmbūlam ।
Mūlādhārādābrahmarandhraparyantaṃ
Brahmarandhrādāmūlādhāraparyantaṃ

Gatāgatarūpeṇa Prādakṣiṇyam । *Turyāvasthā Namaskāraḥ* ।

Dehaśūnyapramātṛtānimajjanaṃ Baliharaṇam ।

Satyamasti Lartavyamakartavyamaudāsīnyanityātmavilāpanaṃ Homaḥ ।

Svayaṃ Tatpādukānimajjanaṃ Paripūrṇadhyānam ।

Evaṃ Muhūrtatrayaṃ (Muhūrtadvitayaṃ Muhūrtamātraṃ Vā)

Bhāvanāparo Jīvanmukto Bhavati Sa Eva Śivayogīti Gadyate ।

Ādimatenāntaścakrabhāvanāḥ ।

Tasya Devatātmaikyasiddhiḥ । *Cintitakāryāṇyayatnena Siddhyanti* ।

Sa Eva Śivayogīti Kathyate । *Kādihādimatoktena Bhāvanā Pratipāditā* ।

Jīvanmukto Bhavati । *Ya Evaṃ Veda* । *Ityupaniṣat* । *(So'tharvaśiro'dhīte* ।*)*

Śānti Mantraḥ ।

Oṃ Bhadraṃ Karṇebhiḥ Śṛṇuyāma Devāḥ ॥

Bhadraṃ Paśyemākṣabhiryajatrāḥ ॥

Sthirairaṅgaistuṣṭuvāg̃Sastanūbhiḥ ॥ *Vyaśema Devahitaṃ Yadāyuḥ* ॥

Svasti Na Indro Vṛddhaśravāḥ ॥ *Svasti Naḥ Pūṣā Viśvavedāḥ* ॥

Svasti Nastārkṣyo Ariṣṭanemiḥ ॥ *Svasti No Bṛhaspatirdadhātu* ॥

Oṃ Śāntiḥ Śāntiḥ Śāntiḥ ॥

Ityatharvaṇavede Bhāvanopaniṣatsampūrṇā ॥

भावनोपनिषत्

शान्ति मन्त्रः

ॐ भद्रं कर्णेभिः शृणुयाम देवाः । भद्रं पश्येमाक्षभिर्यजत्राः ।
स्थिरैरङ्गैस्तुष्टुवाँसस्तनूभिः । व्यशेम देवहितं यदायुः ।
स्वस्ति न इन्द्रो वृद्धश्रवाः । स्वस्ति नः पूषा विश्ववेदाः ।
स्वस्ति नस्ताक्ष्र्यो अरिष्टनेमिः । स्वस्ति नो बृहस्पतिर्दधातु ॥

ॐ शान्तिः शान्तिः शान्तिः॥

हरिः ॐ ।

आत्मानमखण्डमण्डलाकारमवृत्य सकलब्रह्माण्डमण्डलं स्वप्रकाशं ध्यायेत् ।

ॐ श्रीगुरुः सर्वकारणभूता शक्तिः । तेन नवरन्ध्ररूपो देहः । नवशक्तिरूपं श्रीचक्रम् ।
वाराही पितृरूपा । कुरुकुल्ला बलिदेवता माता ।

पुरुषार्थाः सागराः । देहो नवरत्नद्वीपः ।

त्वगादिसप्तधातुभिरनेकैः संयुक्ताः सङ्कल्पाः कल्पतरवः । तेजः कल्पकोद्यानम् ।

रसनया भाव्यमाना मधुराम्लतिक्तकटुकषायलवणभेदाः षड्रसाः षड्तवः क्रियाशक्तिः पीठम् ।

कुण्डलिनी ज्ञानशक्तिर्गृहम् । इच्छाशक्तिर्महात्रिपुरसुन्दरी ।
ज्ञाता होता ज्ञानमग्निः (ज्ञानमर्घ्यम्) ज्ञेयं हविः ।
ज्ञातृ ज्ञान ज्ञेया नाम भेद भावनं श्रीचक्र पूजनम् ।

नियतिसहिताः शृङ्गारादयो नव रसा अणिमादयः ।
कामक्रोधलोभमोहमदमात्सर्यपुण्यपापमया ब्राह्म्याद्यष्टशक्तयः ।
(आधरनवकम् मुद्राशक्तयः ।)

पृथिव्यप्तेजोवाय्वाकाशश्रोत्रत्वक्चक्षुर्जिह्वाघ्राणवाक्पाणिपादपायूपस्थमनोविकाराः
(कामाकर्षिण्यादि) षोडष शक्तयः ।

वचनादानगमनविसर्गानन्दहानो(पादानो)पेक्षा(ख्य) भुद्धयोऽनङ्ग
कुसुमादिशक्तयोऽष्टौ ।

अलम्बुसा कुहूर्विश्वोदरी वरुणा हस्तिजिह्वा यशस्वत्यश्विनी गान्धारी पूषा शङ्खिनी

सरस्वतीडा पिङ्गला सुषुम्ना चेति चतुर्दश नाड्यः ।

सर्वसंक्षोभिण्यादिचतुर्दशारगा देवताः ।

प्राणापानव्यानोदानसमाननागकूर्मकृकरदेवदत्तधनञ्जया इति दश वायवः ।

सर्वसिद्धिप्रदा देव्यो बहिर्दशारगा देवताः ।

एतद्वायुदशकसंसर्गोपाधिभेधेन रेचकपूरकशोषकदाहप्लावका
(रेचकः पाचकः शोषको दाहकः प्लावका इति)
प्राणमुख्यत्वेन पञ्चधोऽस्ति (जठराग्निर्भवति) ।

क्षारको दारकः क्षोभको मोहको जृम्भक इत्यपालनमुख्यत्वेन पञ्चविधोऽस्ति ।

तेन मनुष्याणां मोहको दाहको (नागप्राधान्येन पञ्चबिधास्ते मनुष्याणां देहगा)

भक्ष्यभोज्यशोष्यलेह्यपेयात्मकं चतुर्विधमन्नं (पञ्चविधमन्नं) पाचयति ।

एता दश वह्निकलाः सर्वज्ञत्वाद्यन्तर्दशारगा देवताः ।

शीतोष्णसुखदुःखेच्छासत्त्वरजस्तमोगुणा वशिन्यादिशक्तयोऽष्तौ ।

शब्दस्पर्शरूपरसगन्धाः पञ्चतन्मात्राः पञ्चपुष्पबाणा मन इक्षुधनुः ।

वश्यो वाणो रागः पाशः । द्वेषोऽङ्कुशः ।

अव्यक्तमहत्तत्त्वमहदहङ्कार इति कामेश्वरी-वज्रेश्वरी भगमालिन्योऽन्त
त्रिकोणाग्रगा देवताः

(निरुपाधिकसंविदेव कामेश्वर। सदानन्दपूर्ण स्वात्मेव परदेवता ललिता।

लौहित्यमेतस्य सर्वस्य विमर्श। अनन्यचित्तत्वेन च सिद्धिः।
भावनायाः क्रिया उपचरः। अहं त्वमस्ति नास्ति कर्तव्यमकर्तव्यमुपासितव्यमिति विकल्पानामात्मनि विलापनम् होमः भवनाविषयाणामभेदभवना तर्पणम्।)

पञ्चदशतिथिरूपेण कालस्य परिणामावलोकनस्थितिः पञ्चदशनित्याः।

श्रद्धानुरूपा धीर्देवता। तयोः कामेश्वरी सदानन्दघना परिपूर्णस्वात्मैक्यरूपा देवता।

सलिलमिति लौहित्यकारणं सत्त्वम्। कर्तव्यमकर्तव्यमिति भावनायुक्त उपचारः।

अस्ति नास्तीति कर्तव्यतानूपचारः।

बाह्याभ्यन्तःकरणानां रूपग्रहणयोग्यतास्त्वित्यावाहनम्।

तस्य बाह्याभ्यन्तःकरणानामेकरूपविषयग्रहणमासनम्।

रक्तशुक्लपदैकीकरणं पाद्यम्। उज्ज्वलदामोदानन्दासनदानमर्घ्यम्।

स्वच्छं स्वतःसिद्धमित्याचमनीयम्। चिच्चन्द्रमयीति सर्वाङ्गस्रवणं स्नानम्।

चिदग्निस्वरूपपरमानन्दशक्तिस्फुरणं वस्त्रम्।

प्रत्येकं सप्तविंशतिधा भिन्नत्वेनेच्छाज्ञान
क्रियात्मकब्रह्मग्रन्थिमद्रसतन्तुब्रह्मनाडी ब्रह्मसूत्रम्।

स्वव्यतिरिक्तवस्तुसङ्गरहितस्मरणां विभूषणम्।

सच्चित्सुखपरिपूर्णतास्मरणं गन्धः।
समस्तविषयाणां मनसः स्थैर्येणानुसंधानं कुसुमम्।

तेषामेव सर्वदा स्वीकरणं धूपः।
पवनावच्छिन्नोर्ध्वज्वलनसच्चिदुल्काकाशदेहो दीपः।

समस्तयातायातवर्ज्यं नैवेद्यम्। अवस्थात्रयाणामेकीकरणं ताम्बूलम्।

मूलाधारादाब्रह्मरन्ध्रपर्यन्तं ब्रह्मरन्ध्रादामूलाधारपर्यन्तं गतागतरूपेण प्रादक्षिण्यम्।

तुर्यावस्था नमस्कारः । देहशून्यप्रमातृतानिमज्जनं बलिहरणम् ।

सत्यमस्ति लर्तव्यमकर्तव्यमौदासीन्यनित्यात्मविलापनं होमः ।

स्वयं तत्पादुकानिमज्जनं परिपूर्णध्यानम् ।

एवं मुहूर्तत्रयं (मुहूर्तद्वितयं मुहूर्तमात्रं वा) भावनापरो जीवन्मुक्तो भवति स एव शिवयोगीति गद्यते ।

आदिमतेनान्तश्चक्रभावनाः । तस्य देवतात्मैक्यसिद्धिः ।

चिन्तितकार्याण्ययत्नेन सिद्ध्यन्ति । स एव शिवयोगीति कथ्यते ।

कादिहादिमतोक्तेन भावना प्रतिपादिता । जीवन्मुक्तो भवति ।

य एवं वेद । इत्युपनिषत् । (सोऽथर्वशिरोऽधीते ।)

शान्ति मन्त्र:

ॐ भद्रं कर्णेभिः शृणुयाम देवाः । भद्रं पश्येमाक्षभिर्यजत्राः ।
स्थिरैरङ्गैस्तुष्टुवाँसस्तनूभिः । व्यशेम देवहितं यदायुः ।
स्वस्ति न इन्द्रो वृद्धश्रवाः । स्वस्ति नः पूषा विश्ववेदाः ।
स्वस्ति नस्ताक्ष्योर्ं अरिष्टनेमिः । स्वस्ति नो बृहस्पतिर्दधातु ॥

ॐ शान्तिः शान्तिः शान्तिः॥

*****

About the Author

(http://Ramamurthy.jaagruti.co.in)

Dr. Ramamurthy is a versatile personality having experience and expertise in various areas of Banking, related IT solutions, Information Security, IT Audit, Vedas, Samskrutam and so on.

His thirst for continuous learning does not subside. Even at the age of late fifties, he did research on a unique topic "Information Technology and Samskrutam" and obtained Ph.D. – doctorate degree from University of Madras. He is into a project of developing a Samskrutam based compiler.

It is his passion to spread his knowledge and experience through conducting classes, training programmes and writing books.

He has already published books as detailed below. Further books are in pipe-line.

#	Title	Remarks	Pages
		Indology Related	
1.	*Shrī Lalita Sahasranāmam*	English translation of Shrī *Bhāskararāya's Bhāśyam*	750
2.	Power of *Shrī Vidyā*	The secrets demystified – with lucid English rendering and commentaries	80
3.	ஸ்ரீ வித்யையின் ஶக்தி	ஸ்ரீ வித்யா ரகசியங்கள்	100
4.	*Samatā* – **समता**	An exposition of Similarities in *Lalita Sahasranāma* with *Soundaryalaharī, Saptaśatī, Viśṇu Sahasranāma* and *Shrīmad Bhagavad Gīta*	172
5.	ஸமதா – **समता**	ஸ்ரீ லலிதா ஸஹஸ்ரநாமம் ஸௌந்தர்யலஹரீ, ஸப்தஶதீ, ஸ்ரீ விஷ்ணு ஸஹஸ்ரநாமம் மற்றும் ஸ்ரீமத் பகவத் கீதைகளில் ஒற்றுமையின் ஒரு வெளிப்பாடு	266
6.	*Advaita* in *Shākta*	Advaita Philosophy discussed in Shakta related Books	80
7.	*Shrī Lalitā Triśatī*	300 divine names of the celestial Mother – **English** translation of *Shrī Ādhi Śaṅkara's Bhāśyam*	193
8.	ஸ்ரீ லலிதா த்ரிஶதி	300 divine names of the celestial Mother – Tamil translation of *Shrī Ādi Śaṅkara's Bhāśyam*	234
9.	Secrets of *Mahāśakti*	Chandi demystified	78
10.	*Daśa Mahā Vidyā*	Ten cosmic forms of the Divine mother	60

#	Title	Remarks	Pages
11.	ஸ்ரீ வித்யா பேதங்கள்	ஸ்ரீவித்யா உபாசனையின் படிகள் - கோவை ஶதச் சண்டீ மலர்	51
12.	*Shrīvidya* Variances	Variances in Srividya Upasana	50
13.	ஸ்ரீ தேவீ ஸ்துதிகள்	பல முக்கிய அம்பாள் ஸ்தோத்ரங்கள்	133
14.	Śrī Devī Stutis – श्री देवी स्तुतिः	Various important stotras of Sri Devi	223
15.	ஷண்மத மந்த்ரங்கள்	பொள்ளாச்சி ஸ்ரீ ஸஹஸ்ரசண்டீ மஹாயாக நினைவு மலர்	145
16.	*Śanmata Mantras* – षण्मत मन्त्राः	Important Mantras relating to Gods of six religions	87
17.	தேவதா மந்த்ரங்கள்	அக்கரைப்பட்டி ஸஹஸ்ரசண்டீ மஹாயாக நினைவு மலர்	32
18.	ஆதி ஶங்கரரும் ஷண்மதமும்	ஷண்மதங்களைப் பற்றிய ஒரு அறிமுகம்	32
19.	ஸ்ரீ ஷண்மத தேவதா அர்ச்சனை	ஸ்ரீ மஹா கும்பாபிஷேக மலர்	64
20.	*Vaidhīka* Wedding	Typical Wedding process in English	56
21.	வைதீகத் திருமணம்	Typical Wedding process in Tamil	57
22.	ஸ்ரீகுரு பாத பூஜா விதானம்	சித்தகிரி ஸஹஸ்ரசண்டீ மலர்	44
23.	குரு வார வழிபாடு		70
24.	ஸ்ரீவித்யா ஷடாம்னாய மந்த்ரங்கள்	சித்தகிரி ஸஹஸ்ரசண்டீ மலர்	60
25.	*Ekatā*	Oneness among Shiva, Vishnu and Shakti	277
26.	ஏகதா - एकता	ஶிவபெருமான், விஷ்ணு மற்றும் ஶக்திக்குள் ஒற்றுமை	370
27.	*Vedas* – An Analytical Perspective	A description of Veda, Vedanta, Vedanga, Jyotisha, Shastra, etc.	240
28.	வேதங்கள் - ஒரு பகுப்பாய்வு	A description of Veda, Vedanta, Vedanga, Jyotisha, Shastra, etc.	280
29.	பரமாச்சார்யாள் நோக்கில் ஸ்ரீ லலிதாம்பிகா	The explanation given by Paramacharya on some of the names in Lalita Sahasranama	175
30.	*Ṣaṇṇavati Tarpaṇa*	Repaying Debts to Ancestors	42
31.	ஷண்ணவதி தர்பணம்	முன்னோர் கடன் தீர்த்தல்	48
32.	*Shrī Mahā Pratyangirā Devī*	Holy Divine mother in ferocious form	41
33.	ஸ்ரீ மஹா ப்ரத்யங்கிரா தேவீ	தெய்வீக அன்னையின் பயங்கர வடிவம்	51
34.	*Śrī Chakra Navāvarṇam*	Marvels of *Śrī Chakra*	115
35.	ஸ்ரீ சக்ர நவாவர்ணம்	ஸ்ரீ சக்ரத்தின் அதிசயங்கள்	130
36.	அம்பிகையின் (திரு) அவதாரங்கள்	ஸ்ரீ தேவியின் பல்வேறு அவதாரங்கள்	142

#	Title	Remarks	Pages
37.	Incarnations of Holy Mother	Different Incarnations of *Śrī Devī*	140
38.	ஸ்ரீ பிரணவானந்தர் - ஒரு சரிதம்	ஒரு அரிய ஸ்வாமிகளின் திவ்ய சரிதம்	121
39.	ஸன்யாஸம் - ஓர் அலசல்	ஹிந்து மத ஸன்யாஸ பேதங்கள் - ஒரு பகுப்பாய்வு	140
40.	Asceticism – an Analysis	A Study of Hindu *Sanyasam*	140
41.	ஶாந்தமும் ப்ரணவமும்	(ஸ்ரீ ஶாந்தானந்தரும் ஸ்ரீ ப்ரணவானந்தரும்) குரு சிஷ்யருக்கு உபதேசங்கள்	120
42.	ஸ்ரீ ஸஹஸ்ராக்ஷரீ வித்யா	2020 சாதுர்மாஸ்ய மலர்	84
43.	*Shakta Upanishats*	*Upanishats* about *Sri Devi*	385
44.	ஶாக்த உபநிஷதங்கள்	*Upanishats* about *Sri Devi*	400
45.	ஸ்ரீ **தேவீ கீதை**	Sri Devi Geeta	194
46.	*Śrī Devī Gīta*	Sri Devi Geeta	180
47.	*Śrī Gāyatrī Sahasranamam*	1,000 Divine Names of *Śrī Gāyatrī Mātā*	392
48.	ஸ்ரீ **காயத்ரீ** ஸஹஸ்ரநாமம்	ஸ்ரீ **காயத்ரி** மாதாவின்1,000 திவ்ய நாமங்கள்	450
49.	ஸ்ரீ ஸௌந்தர்யலஹரீ	ஸௌந்தர்யலஹரீ ஒரு உள்-அறிவு	250
50.	*Śrī Soundaryalaharī*	*Soundaryalaharī* an Insight	200
51.	*Śrī Vārāhī Devī*	Holy Divine Mother with a hog face	96
52.	ஸ்ரீ வாராஹீ தேவீ	பன்றி முகத்துடன் கூடிய புனிதத் தெய்வீக அன்னை	106
53.	Śrī Vijaya Bhairavar	A Terrifying, Sacred, Divine form of Lord Shiva	164
54.	ஸ்ரீ விஜய பை₄ரவர்	ஶிவபெருமானின் ஒரு திகிலூட்டும் புனித தெய்வீக உருவம்	188
55.	ஸ்ரீ ப₄த்₃ர காளீ	ஸ்ரீ தேவியின் ஒரு திகிலூட்டும் புனித தெய்வீக உருவம்	226
56.	*Śrī Bhadra Kālī*	A Startling, Sacred and Divine form of *Śrī Devī*	224
57.	ஸ்ரீ தாரா – நீல ஸரஸ்வதீ	2nd Devi of Dasha Maha Vidya	182
58.	*Śrī Tārā Devī* – Blue *Saraswatī*	2nd Devi of Dasha Maha Vidya	174
59.	*Śrī Tripura Sundarī Devī*	3rd Devi of Dasha Maha Vidya	200
60.	ஸ்ரீ த்ரிபுர சுந்தரீ தேவீ	3rd Devi of Dasha Maha Vidya	200
61.	*Chaṇḍī Homa Vidhānam*	Process of performing Chandi Homam	80
62.	சண்டீ ஹோம விதானம்	Process of performing Chandi Homam	80
	Applied Samskrutam Based		
63.	*Paribhāshā Stora—s*	An exploration of *Lalita Sahasranāmam*	96
64.	பரிபாஷா ஸ்தோத்ரங்கள்	ஸ்ரீ லலிதா ஸஹஸ்ரநாமம் - ஒரு ஆய்வு	135
65.	*Shrī Cakra*, An Esoteric Approach	Mathematical Construction to draw *Shrī Cakra*	64

#	Title	Remarks	Pages
66.	ஸ்ரீ சக்கரம் வரையும் முறை	ஸ்ரீ சக்கரம் வரைய கணித கட்டுமானம்	84
67.	Number System in Samskrutam	An overview of Mathematics based on Samskrutam	123
68.	ஸமஸ்க்ருதத்தில் எண்ணியல்	ஸமஸ்க்ருதத்தில் பொதிந்துள்ள எண் கணிதம்	140
69.	*Vedic* Mathematics	30 formulae elucidated	146
70.	Vedic IT	Information Technology and Samskrutam	162
	IT Based		
71.	Orthogonal Array	A Statistical Tool for Software Testing	180
	Banking Based		
72.	Retail Banking	A guide book for Novice	213
73.	Corporate Banking	A guide book for Novice	232
74.	Dictionary of Financial Terms	A Guide Book for all – Demystifying Myriad Global Financial Terms	215
75.	GRC in BFS Industry	(**G**overnance, **R**isk Management and **Co**mpliance by Banking & Finance Industry)	200

*****

Made in the USA
Las Vegas, NV
13 May 2023

72015951R00036